Swi

C000242153

A guide to recent architecture

...

Maya Huber and Thomas Hildebrand

Switzerland

A guide to recent architecture

● ● ● ellipsis

•••

PUBLISHED BY •••ellipsis
2 Rufus Street London N1 6PE
E MAIL ...@ellipsis.co.uk
www http://www.ellipsis.com

COPYRIGHT © 2001 ellipsis london limited

ISBN 1 84166 006 X
PRINTING AND BINDING Hong Kong

•••ellipsis is a trademark of Ellipsis
London Limited

For a copy of the Ellipsis catalogue or
information on special quantity orders
of Ellipsis books please contact
Faye Chang (0)20 7739 3157 or
faye@ellipsis.co.uk)

Maya Huber and Thomas Hildebrand 2001

Contents

Introduction

Switzerland's image has always been closely linked to unspoilt nature and efficient service industries. It is, therefore, no wonder that it has attracted more people in search of steep mountainsides dotted with wooden chalets and grazing cows than seekers of avant-garde architecture. And yet, the last two decades have seen a hitherto unparalleled production of innovative buildings. The quality of recent architecture in Switzerland, in combination with the phenomenon of cultural consumerism, has pushed many projects to the centre of popular attention: Peter Zumthor's thermal bath in Vals (page 5.52), Vitra's architectural themepark at Weil am Rhein just over the border in Germany (pages 2.2–8), Mario Botta's Tinguely Museum in Basel (page 1.26) and Jean Nouvel's Kultur- und Kongresshaus in Lucerne (page 7.4), to name only a few. Every year these sites attract thousands of visitors in search of an architectural experience. In the 1990s, Swiss architects such as Herzog & de Meuron and Zumthor have come to be regarded as among the main proponents of the international avant-garde as they address some of the most hotly debated issues in contemporary architecture.

The minimalist box

From the outside, Swiss architecture, and in particular the newer buildings in the German-speaking part of the country, appear simple and sober. Its simplicity is, however, also its enigma. Firmly placed into the ground without base and devoid of any loud spatial contraptions, this architecture avoids spectacular semiotic form-giving. A discreet immediacy of materials, a firm belief in technology and a recognition of the banal are much more central than artifice, collage or even irony. Articulating neither front nor back, nor referring to the human scale, the underlying focus often lies on the material. This self-referentiality can be problematic when the relationship to the context is too subtle or when mere reduction is regarded as an architectural solution in itself.

The Swiss affinity to the box is seemingly grounded in an embarrassment of riches. This finds its roots in Calvinist puritanism and the heritage of a largely agrarian life. Wealth in the country is rarely displayed outwardly; rather, it manifests itself in a discreet understatement cherishing quality and precision. Whereas 'simple' often carries the connotation of 'cheap' elsewhere, in Switzerland 'simple' is often understood as being very expensive.

At first glance the labels 'new simplicity' or 'new minimalism' are easy and convenient to use, satisfying a need to group and classify. This classification is, however, much contested by insiders who fiercely denounce the oversimplification of a seeming uniformity: some focus on tectonic and structural clarity (Meili & Peter, Diener & Diener), others pursue new ways in the application of prefabricated components (Burkhalter & Sumi, Gigon & Guyer). Zumthor concentrates on craftsmanship and the atmospheric qualities of natural materials. Herzog & de Meuron go a step further even, and question materiality itself by continuously thematising perceptions of the surface.

Utilitarian modernism

The Swiss are to a certain extent more comfortable with the modern movement than their neighbours. Not having been directly involved in the historic upheavals of the twentieth century, Switzerland does not suffer the ideological taint and dogmatism associated with modernism, which elsewhere has resulted in the movement's rejection. The utilitarian aspect of the modern movement fell on fertile soil as it reflected the needs of Swiss culture in the early twentieth century. Looking for the roots of recent architecture in Switzerland reveals the ideology of the *Neues Bauen* of the 1930s – a movement that influenced the laying out of the foundations for the development of a modified modernism under the influence of regional traditions.

In the decades following the second world war, Switzerland experienced rapid economic growth in which more agricultural land was transformed into suburban and industrial estates. Atelier 5's visionary Halen housing estate (from 1961) was ahead of its time in an era less concerned with optimising land resources than with profiting from the economic boom. This period, which reached its climax in the political unrest of 1968, led to a crisis in architecture that was clearly felt in the architectural schools, where increasing emphasis was placed on sociopolitical aspects. It was in the early 1970s that the Federal Institute of Technology (ETH) in Zürich gained in international reputation with teachers such as Bernhard Hoesli, Luigi Snozzi, Dolf Schnebli and especially Aldo Rossi, who worked towards reasserting the autonomy of architecture. These mentors were of great influence on a whole generation of architects then studying in Zürich: Jacques Herzog, Pierre de Meuron, Roger Diener, Daniele Marques and Christian Sumi, among others.

The mid-1970s saw the emergence of a strong new movement out from Italian-speaking Ticino – the *Tendenza*. For the first time since Halen, Swiss architecture stood in the international limelight. A group exhibition at the ETH entitled 'Tendenzen', which introduced the works of young Ticinesi architects, met with great interest. Mario Botta, Mario Campi & Franco Pessina, Aurelio Galfetti, Flora Ruchat-Roncati, Luigi Snozzi and Livio Vacchini were major protagonists of this new movement, which combined various types of Italian-influenced rationale with traditional regional architecture.

In the 1980s it was the teachings of Fabio Reinhart and Miroslav Šik's Analogue Architecture at the ETH that attracted much attention. Their approach to anonymous and regionally rooted architecture helped raise awareness of the everyday, and tried to capture the significance and atmosphere of a place. Many of the younger Grison architects – such as Andrea Deplazes, Dieter Jüngling and Valerio Olgiati – studied with these professors and a great sensitivity for place is characteristic of their work.

From the mid-1980s, international attention gradually shifted from Ticino in the south to the German-speaking north, now the principal centre of architectural activity.

Groomed nature and civilised engineering

Nature is Switzerland's most impressive feature, but besides the untamed and harsh mountain peaks of the Alps, Swiss nature is anything but natural: virtually every patch is cultivated and perfectly groomed. Such exceptional care is also devoted to a building culture strongly rooted in regional traditions. It reinforces the widespread image of a neat and tidy land – city centres and mountain villages alike. The remoteness of certain areas has contributed to this rich variety of distinct regional traditions, reflected in the formal articulation, materiality and construction techniques used – such as the wooden chalet in the Valais, the stately Bernese farmhouse, or the stout, white houses in the Engadin.

What endows even the remotest area with a sense of contemporaneity is the way in which all of Switzerland is bound into a tightly controlled infrastructure, within easy and comfortable reach by means of roads, trains, postal buses or chairlifts. This accessibility and efficiency is the result of a long history of sophisticated civil engineering. The motorways,

Introduction

bridges, hydroelectric dams, tunnels and the odd military fortification have over time become an integral part of the landscape. The influence on architecture of engineers such as Robert Maillart or Christian Menn is undisputed, and there have been several fruitful collaborations between architects and civil engineers in recent years, such as the Sunniberg bridge (page 5.6), the wooden bridge in Nesslau (page 4.14) or the Transjurane motorway (page 9.2).

Building culture

To this day, architecture in Switzerland is not a protected profession and anyone may call him- or herself an architect and set up practice. At the same time it is still a much broader and better-paid profession than in many other countries. Traditionally, architects not only design a building, but also do the working drawings, measure quantities and estimate costs. In most cases it is also the architects themselves who act as main contractors, responsible for the subcontractors and the supervision of construction. This, in combination with the strong tradition and appreciation of craftsmanship, has made it possible to sustain extremely high standards in construction. Emphatic concern for the means of assembly and a great sensibility for materials thus make possible the quality and precision of construction – characteristics cherished and unique to the country.

While much of Europe saw a general collapse of confidence in both architects and architecture in the 1980s, the traditional cultural status of the profession in Switzerland remained unchanged. For good and for ill, placidity and protectionism have nurtured economic growth and have kept the building industry stable for a long time. Recent years, however, have seen changes in the comprehensive role Swiss architects used to play in the building process. Feeling the impacts of the 1990s' recession later than their colleagues in other countries, many architects in Switzerland are nevertheless struggling to come to terms with the socio-economic changes. As elsewhere, the economic aspect of building has become ever more important, and architects are struggling not to be replaced by general contractors in order to keep their tight control of the design and construction process.

Commodifying architecture

All the more interesting is the phenomenon of the 'star-architect' – suddenly architects and their buildings are illustrated in popular magazines. Architects have become cultural ambassadors and while no popular newspaper or magazine would have written at length about architecture 20 years ago, it is now a topic cool enough to be regularly featured in both glossy and academic magazines. Employing architecture to display civic pride or to consolidate positions of power is nothing new. What is remarkable, however, is that architects do not disappear behind the project or client any longer. On the contrary, clients or cities are now using architects' names for advertising purposes. Rolf Fehlbaum, the managing director of Vitra Furniture Design Company, was one of the first in Switzerland (and Europe) to see the potential of architecture in corporate identity. Not only collecting chairs, Fehlbaum has also since 1982 set out to collect buildings by famous international architects, such as Frank Gehry, Zaha Hadid, Nicholas Grimshaw, Alvaro Siza or Tadao Ando – a strategy that has made Vitra a much-quoted textbook example of successful corporate identity. This in turn has had the effect of promoting 'trademark' architecture, buildings that carry the easily recognisable signature of an architect, be it Botta, Gehry or Richard Meier. The culture industry is thriving, but while much contemporary visual or performing arts seem accessible to insiders only, architecture has become part of mainstream popular culture. With economic pressure on the architect, the middle ground making up the solid cultural base is at risk of becoming polarised into star- and non-architecture.

This guide highlights some new and innovative approaches to architecture that offer alternatives to sprawling non-architecture and the usual houses catering for dreams of an idyllic rural heritage. Contrary to a reputation of being backward and conservative, it is often in remote villages that some of the most refreshing examples of the new architecture are to be found. Without falling into nostalgia, many projects are well-integrated and refer to older building traditions and local resources, while at the same time exploring the advantages of contemporary technology.

ACKNOWLEDGEMENTS

Many people have made this book possible in different ways. We would like to thank all the architects and critics who generously supplied material and found the time to discuss their work. Among the many we pestered for information and advice we are particularly grateful to Alain Roserens, but also Christoph Sättler and Frances Hsu with whom we spent many hours discussing architecture; Frances, Simone Kubli and Thomas Olver all were an invaluable help with the proofreading and finishing of the first draft; thanks to Katarina Lütscher and all the other photographers who kindly provided their materials. Thanks to Swiss Tourism London, especially Eveline Lafone, who supported our travels through Switzerland and Pro Helvetia for their financial support. Finally we would like to express our gratitude to Tom Neville at Ellipsis for his commitment to this book.

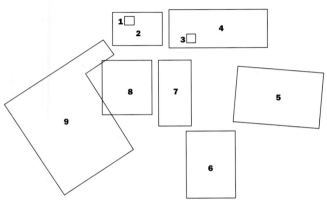

1 Basel
2 Greater Basel
3 Zürich
4 Greater Zürich
5 Grison
6 Ticino
7 Central Switzerland
8 Bern and region
9 Romandie

Using this book

This guide divides Switzerland's 26 cantons and half-cantons into nine architectural regions. The projects are grouped around several centres. Some correspond to cantons or cities, such as Basel or Zürich, while others are based on general, sometimes overlapping, boundaries. Travelling in Switzerland is easy and most of the objects included in this book can be efficiently reached by public transport: trains connect most cities and the yellow-coloured postal buses reach even the remotest village. Switzerland is quadrilingual (Swiss-German, French, Italian and Romansch) but you will find that most people also speak some English.

Many important recent contributions to Swiss architecture are in fact private homes, and have not been included for reasons of privacy. Free, or at least limited, public access was an important determining factor in selecting the buildings for this book. The task of selecting was difficult and the final choice, of course, subjective. We are therefore always grateful for information on other interesting objects worth seeing.

Architecture galleries and museums

There is an increasing number of galleries and museums devoted to architecture. Check with these institutes for forthcoming events:

Basel: Architekturmuseum, Pfluggässlein 3, 4001 Basel (041 61261 14 13); www.architekturmuseum.ch

Bern: Architekturforum Bern, Kapellenstrasse 14, 3001 Bern (031 390 25 83); www.architekturforum-bern.ch

Lausanne: Ecole Polytéchnique Fédéral de Lausanne, Department d'Architécture, Avenue de l'Eglise Anglais 12, 1006 Lausanne (021 693 32 31)

Lucerne: Architekturgalerie Luzern Moosstrasse 2, 6006 Lucerne (041 24920 18)

St Gallen: Architekturforum Ostschweiz, Davidstrasse 40, 9004 St Gallen; tel.: 071 222 07 11 (371 24 11)

Zürich: Architekturforum Zürich, Neumarkt 15, 8001 Zürich (01 252 92 95)

Institut GTA, Eidg. Technische Hochschule Hönggerberg HI, C75 Einsteinstrasse, 8093 Zürich (01 633 28 97) (Tuesday to Thursday)

Weil-am-Rhein, Germany: Vitra Design Museum, Charles Eames Strasse 1, D-79576 Weil-am-Rhein (0049 7621 702 37 20); www.design-museum.de

Swiss architecture journals

Werk, Bauen & Wohnen
archithese
Hochparterre
Faces
revista technica

Guidebooks

Modern Architecture Itineraries in Ticino (Itinerari di architettura), Ticino Turismo, 1989 (free, available at tourist offices in Ticino)

Brown-Manrique, Gerardo, *The Ticino Guide*, Princeton Architectural Press, New York 1989

Burckhardt, Daniel and Daniel Wittlin, *Architekturführer Basel: ein Führer zur Architektur in Basel und Umgebung 1980–1993*, Wiese, Basel 1993

Daguerre, Mercedes, *Birkhäuser Architectural Guide: Switzerland*,

Birkhäuser, Basel 1997

Disch, Peter, *Architettura recentese nel Ticino/Neuere Architektur im Tessin, 1980–1995*, ADV, Lugano 1996

Architektur in der Deutschen Schweiz 1980–1990, ADV, Lugano 1992

Gantenbein, Köbi, *Bauen in Graubünden: ein Führer zur Gegenwartsarchitektur,* 2nd edn, Hochparterre, Zürich 1999

Honig, Roderick and Benedikt Loderer, *La Romandie Existe. Un guide de l'architecture contemporaine. Ein Führer zur Gegenwartsarchitektur,* Hochparterre, Zürich 1998

Huber, Dorothee, *Architekturführer Basel: die Baugeschichte der Stadt und ihrer Umgebung*, Architekturmuseum Basel, Basel 1993

Koch, Ursula *et al.* (eds), *Architektur in Zürich 1980–1990: eine Auswahl von 100 Objekten,* Bauamt II der Stadt Zürich, Zürich 1990

Kommission für Kunst und Architektur des Kt. Bern (ed.), *100 Bauten im Kanton Bern: ein Architekturführer*, Benteli, Bern 1992

Windhofel, Lutz, *Drei Länder, eine Stadt: neueste Bauten im grenzübergreifenden Stadtraum Basel 1992–97*, Birkhauser, Basel 1997

Zeller, Christa (ed.), *SchweizerArchitekturführer*, vols I–III, Werk, Zürich 1996 (German/French/English)

Books and exhibition catalogues

Achleitner, Friedrich, *Neues Bauen in den Alpen*, Architekturmuseum Basel, Basel 1999

Mayr Fingerle, Christoph (ed.), *Neues Bauen in den Alpen*, Architekturmuseum Basel, Basel 1996

Burkle, J Christoph (ed.), *Junge Schweizer Architekten/Young Swiss Architects*, Niggli, Heiden 1997

Gilbert, Mark and Kevin Alter (eds), *Construction, Intention, Detail: Five*

Projects of Five Swiss Architects, Artemis, Zürich 1994

Humbel, Carmen, *Junge Schweizer Architekten und Architektinnen/ Young Swiss Architects*, Artemis, Zürich 1995

Werner, Frank and Sabine Schneider, *Neue Tessiner Architektur. Perspektiven einer Utopie*, Deutsche Verlags-Anstalt, Stuttgart 1990

Basel

Signal box, Auf dem Wolf

The signal box, a key work in Herzog & de Meuron's œuvre, needs little introduction. The tall, copper volume sits right on the edge of the railway tracks next to the new engine depot (page 1.6) and an old cemetery. The building's concrete shell contains electronic equipment to control signals to the depot and the adjoining tracks. The six-storey volume is fully wrapped with 20-centimetre-wide protective copper strips, the coiling twisted upwards in certain areas to allow daylight to enter the windows below. Comparisons with a Faraday cage are inevitable, if not welcome, even though this protection is unnecessary since all the equipment is already adequately shielded.

The signal box evades an easy grasp. It infiltrates our perception as it constantly changes its appearance, depending on light and weather conditions, our own movement and the weathering process. The indeterminate scale and the texture of this seemingly trivial monolith do not fail to intrigue and charm (one) time and again. The true nature of this archaic and very sculptural monolith can only be understood through experience.

MH/TH In a time characterised by the fast pace of quickly changing images generated by the electronic media, has it also become more important for architecture to draw attention to itself by making a stronger visual impact?

Jacques Herzog Architecture cannot measure itself with the electronic media. The developments in that field are progressing at an incredible pace. The TV screen will always have a more fascinating and sharper quality, but only on a two-dimensional level. If architecture wants to play a significant role in the future, it has to rely on its own qualities, it needs to exploit fully its own potential. Architecture needs to develop new strategies of images, subversive strategies, which raise questions

Herzog & de Meuron Architekten, AG 1992–95

Basel

Herzog & de Meuron Architekten, AG 1992–95

rather than satisfy superfluous needs in the way TV does. If we can keep the kind of architecture that appeals to the different senses alive, then architecture will survive.

MH/TH ... so it doesn't always have to be the visual sense that is appealed to? Could you also imagine designing a project generated by a smell?

JH ... we don't take any particular sense as a source for our designs. We would like to make an architecture that appeals to all senses. A complex system of perception is a main characteristic of human existence. Actually, smell has little chance of being integrated into architecture. What we have is the opportunity to work with mass, with solid and heavy elements, not just with flighty images. We can work with the tactile, which is very important to us. ... The better architecture is, the more it fascinates the human being: it touches, moves and flirts with us. It can sharpen our senses, make us more perceptive.

A second, more recent signal box has been finished near the main train station at Münchensteinerbrücke.

ADDRESS Walkenweg/Güterbahnhof Wolf, 4052 Basel
CLIENT Schweizerische Bundesbahnen Hochbau Kreis II
STRUCTURAL ENGINEERING Proplan Ing. AG, Basel
COST SF6.17 million
SIZE 1893 square metres
TRAIN any train from main station
TRAM 10, 11 to Wolfgottesacker
BUS 36 to Dreispitz
ACCESS none; visible from the street

Basel

Herzog & de Meuron Architekten, AG 1992–95

Signal box, Auf dem Wolf

Basel

Herzog & de Meuron Architekten, AG 1992–95

Railway engine depot, Auf dem Wolf

The engine depot is part of an overall renovation programme for the main train station of Basel and is composed of a series of linearly aligned buildings, containing the depot, workshop sheds and a three-storey office block.

The depot and the adjoining signal box (page 1.2) were realised in a first construction phase on a void in the centre of the city characterised by the extensive system of railway tracks flowing largely unnoticed through the urban landscape. Positioned on a small, triangular site amid the tracks, a shrubby architectural biotope has developed – warehouses, depots, sheds, an adjoining cemetery – as well as bushes and weeds.

The hangars of the new depot are aligned in such a way that they optimise the shape of the site. A simple structural system based on cast, *in-situ* concrete walls and a roof structure of one-storey-high steel girders for the skylights take up the geometric pattern of the railtracks: a juxtaposition of different rectangular volumes laid length- and cross-wise. This additive, non-hierarchical system is the building's driving force and its minimalist structure is imbued with a strong sculptural expression.

ADDRESS Walkenweg/Güterbahnhof Wolf, 4052 Basel
CLIENT Schweizerische Bundesbahnen Hochbau Kreis II
STRUCTURAL ENGINEERING Proplan Ing. AG, Basel
COST SF60 million
SIZE 24,550 square metres
TRAM 10, 11 to Wolfgottesacker
BUS 36 to Dreispitz
ACCESS none; visible from the street

Herzog & de Meuron Architekten, AG 1991–95

Herzog & de Meuron Architekten, AG 1991–95

Euregio

It is big and it is white: Euregio confirms all stereotypes and fulfils all expectations commonly associated with Richard Meier's architecture. His trade mark white modernism is masterfully orchestrated around form, light and transparency, while the simple forms and plans are always geometric in nature and follow the classical proportions of the golden section, the circle and the square. Interior spaces are filled with natural light, an impression reinforced by transparency and the whiteness. This building stands out in the cityscape, contrasting strongly with the adjacent buildings.

The high density of buildings by famous architects is impressive – no other city of this size offers such a cast of international stars. This recent addition is prominently located just behind the main train station and opposite the Bankverein training centre, a massive volume built with dark red brick by Diener & Diener. Having just completed the Getty Museum in California, Meier has also made himself a name in Europe where he has realised projects in Barcelona, The Hague and Paris.

ADDRESS Viaduktstrasse 40–44, 4051 Basel
CLIENT Credit Suisse, Bern
STRUCTURAL ENGINEERING Gruner AG, Basel
COST SF80 million
SIZE 20,000 square metres
TRAM 1, 2, 8, 16 to Markthalle
ACCESS by appointment only: contact Karl Braun (061 302 6565)

Richard Meier, Göhner Merkur, AG 1995–98

Basel

Richard Meier, Göhner Merkur, AG 1995–98

SUVA Insurance Building

Investigating the façade as a way of exploring possible permutations in a building's appearance is probably the most important characteristic of projects by Herzog & de Meuron.

When faced with the option of tearing down the old 1950s' administration building of the insurance company, the architects opted to retain and extend the existing structures. Both old and new are covered by a glass membrane: glass strips of different optical and physical qualities enclose the volumes like a second skin. The play of vision and reflection causes a slight, but persistent, disorientation, and the boundaries between the opaque and the transparent are in flux. Depending on the point of view and lighting conditions, the complex either appears as a smooth coherent whole or it reveals its true nature as a conglomerate of two very different volumes beneath the glass. Some of the glass panels bear the silk-screened and endlessly repeated letters 'SUVA', while others are left transparent – a close relationship between old and new is established, not only by the complex's transparency, but also by the repeatedly printed name on the skin. On a practical level, this new skin functions as insulation against weather and acoustical influences. The façade not only manifests the architects' continual concern with the possibilities of the architectural skin, but also satisfies energy-saving requirements. The passer-by experiences the façade as a kind of a barometer – being sensitive to changes in light intensity and temperature, sunlight and heat determine the tilting of the computer-operated panels, giving an open façade in hot weather and a closed one if it is cold.

This unconventional façade manages to endow the disparate parts of the building with a sense of unity, giving the corner building a defined urban presence. The building resists, however, any easy analysis about its underlying structure or interior configuration. Herzog & de Meuron's

Herzog & de Meuron Architekten, AG 1991–93

Herzog & de Meuron Architekten, AG 1991–93

1.12

turn toward a multiple definition of transparency is a departure of considerable significance. Here they have developed an architecture in which definitions are no longer absolute, where appearances must be questioned. The themes addressed in the SUVA building reappear in later works such as the Signal Box (page 1.2) and The Pfaffenholz Sports Centre (page 1.22).

ADDRESS St Jakobstrasse, 4052 Basel
CLIENT Schweizerische Unfallversicherungsgesellschaft, Lucerne
STRUCTURAL ENGINEERING Ingenieurbüro Andreas Zachmann, Basel
(new building); Ingenieurbüro Helmut Pauli, Basel (old building)
COST SF23.25 million
SIZE 8815 square metres
TRAM 1, 3, 8, 10, 11, 14, 15 to Aeschenplatz
ACCESS none; visible from the street

Basel

Herzog & de Meuron Architekten, AG 1991–93

Herzog & de Meuron Architekten, AG 1991–93

Yellow House, Barfüsserplatz

Over the years, Roger Diener has gradually reduced his formal and material vocabulary to an absolute minimum. Today, a Diener & Diener building is nothing but a simple box with solid walls for façades and punched openings for windows.

Situated at the corner of one of Basel's most prominent squares, the bone-dry Yellow House is a perfect example of the skilful application of these few elements on which this architecture relies strongly. The resulting deliberate banality of this highly acclaimed building seems almost insulting. The house is unobtrusive, easily missed or dismissed as having been there for a long time. A reductive aridity paradoxically gives Diener's architecture an openness that ends up being anything but boring.

Working with only two elements, yellow-coloured, fair-faced concrete and a large, rectangular double-window, Diener gives the house a powerful unpretentious appearance. By simply shifting the windows into one of the two possible positions, the observer is more likely to read the individual storey as stressing the corner position or as blending into the street-façade. The aim of the architecture is not to create a fixed composition, but rather to define a set of relationships identifying the building in its particular context.

ADDRESS Steinenvorstadt 2, Kohlenberg 1, 4051 Basel
CLIENT Marcus Diener, Basel
STRUCTURAL ENGINEERING Cyrill Burger & Partner AG, Binningen
SIZE 460 square metres
TRAM 1, 3, 6, 8, 11, 14, 16, 17, to Barfüsserplatz
ACCESS by appointment only

Diener & Diener 1994–95

Basel

Diener & Diener 1994–95

Hotel Teufelhof

The renovated restaurant, gourmet shop, theatre and hotel all retain a classicist appearance; there is even a small archaeological museum in the basement displaying the discoveries made during the building's renovation. Unlike many trendy hotels or restaurants that claim to pursue the interaction of gastronomy and art, the Teufelhof succeeds in a convincing way. When the hotel opened in 1989, eight rooms were offered to invited artists as spaces for installations, the only prerequisite being that the spaces remain usable as bedrooms. Guests cannot escape an immediate confrontation with the art environment in which they spend the night. Those who are willing to do without commonplace hotel furnishing, such as the mini-bar or television, are well rewarded by the unparalleled chance of living intimately within a work of art, an experience hitherto exclusive to the realm of galleries, museums and public spaces. One must not get too attached to a specific room, however, as all eight rooms are changed every 2 or 3 years.

This alternative movement in hotel culture signals a widespread need to escape the anonymous hotel landscape in favour of a stronger individual identity. The Teufelhof has found a way to create an environment in which art and gastronomy can support each other. Profits from the restaurant, wine bar and gourmet shop help to finance the artists' installations and the theatre, which in turn give the Teufelhof its arty image and special atmosphere.

ADDRESS Leonhardsgraben 47–49, 4051 Basel
TRAM 3 to Musikakademie
WEBSITE www.teufelhof.com
ACCESS open; telephone 061 261 1010

M & D Thommy-Kneschaurek 1988–89

Basel

M & D Thommy-Kneschaurek 1988–89

Vogesen School

The new school is an addition to two existing school buildings, both built in the representational style typical of the nineteenth century. The new volume fits effortlessly into the structure of the surroundings and, without renouncing its own independence, allows the reading of the city block as a loosely structured perimeter development.

MH/TH The untrained eye does not notice your buildings … do you mind?

Roger Diener The architecture of a new building is at its best when it manages to enrich a site by uncovering its inherent potential. This happens when a new building opens our eyes to the special qualities of the existing buildings around it. That's why we don't care if our buildings aren't in strong contrast with existing structures. An addition should take on the role of being part of a richer whole. 'Untrained eyes' might not immediately notice an exceptional quality in the new whole, but (at best) they will be astonished gradually to perceive the transformation of a place that hasn't really changed all that much.

MH/TH Why do you explore the disruption of scale or scalelessness – something which can be best observed in your use of large windows?

RD If we design unexpectedly large openings for our windows, we don't do so to disrupt, but to strike a balance between inner and outer spaces. If by doing so we strain people's viewing habits, then that's not bad either … it would be an indication that our buildings are not completely dissolving into the context of the city after all ….

ADDRESS St Johanns-Ring 17, 4056 Basel
STRUCTURAL ENGINEERING Cyrill Burger & Partner AG
TRAM 11 to St Johanns-Tor
ACCESS school hours only: Monday to Friday, 9.00–17.00

Diener & Diener 1993–96

Diener & Diener 1993–96

Luzernerring housing

In close proximity to Herzog & de Meuron's Pfaffenholz Sports Centre stands Michael Alder's block of flats. Part of the larger Luzernerring housing complex, this good and concise example of simple residential housing is aligned with the street while bordering a large allotment.

Alder is a builder much more devoted to problem-solving on a technical and functional level than establishing a role of artist–architect for himself. His architecture is driven by ethical and social aspirations aimed at reasonably priced residential building. Typology, proportion and autonomy of parts have become the fundamental principles of Alder's architecture – that in his view should be simple and quiet.

This block of 98 flats is governed by an aesthetic of necessity. Practical and intelligent layouts are the main characteristics with eight apartments making a housing unit. Bathroom, kitchen and staircase are located along the façade, allowing ample natural light and air to enter. Every apartment has three balconies: two smaller ones facing the street and a long, continuous one at the back. The balconies thus create a volumetric play and rhythmically structure the two façades. A beautiful, 200-metre-long urban promenade on the roof is open to everyone and it offers an uninhibited view over the city.

ADDRESS Bungestrasse 10–18, 4056 Basel
CLIENT Pensionskasse des Basler Stadtpersonals/Neue Wohnbaugenossenschaft, Basel
TRAM 3 to Luzernerring
BUS 36 to Luzernerring
ACCESS none; visible from the street

Alder & Partner 1991–94

Basel

Alder & Partner 1991–94

Pfaffenholz Sports Centre, St Louis

Basel's borderzone has historically been considered an unprestigeous location and home to programmes or institutions such as cemeteries, allotments or psychiatric clinics. Situated within this zone, right on the Swiss–French border, lies the Pfaffenholz Sports Centre, used by people from both countries. The low and clear-cut cube is clad with dark glass panels and alludes to an elegant industrial architecture – as anonymous as the no man's land it occupies.

The giant sports hall with its surrounding gallery for spectators, marks the centre of the main volume. Attached to it is a narrow concrete block containing changing rooms and service functions. Its canopy shelters the main entrance and the doors leading to the individual locker rooms.

The invention of imprinting photographic pictures onto a concrete surface was first used for this complex. The repeated image, which is in fact a photograph of the very gravel the concrete is made of, creates a spatial effect which dissolves the material's solidity. The printed prefabricated panels make up floor, wall and roof of the covered area in front of the changing rooms and the abstract stone pattern alludes to the leaves of the surrounding trees, thereby drawing nature into the man-made space.

Simultaneously the theme of imprinting on glass, was taken up again and applied on the dark smoke glass covering the large central hall. The glass, imprinted with the image of the insulation mats lying underneath, undergoes in effect a similar defamiliarisation as the concrete, which brings the two materials into a new relationship.

MH/TH Is it a coincidence that in a time when tattoos are back en vogue, you are 'tattooing' your buildings?

Jacques Herzog We think that the present-day preoccupation with the

Herzog & de Meuron Architekten, AG 1992–93

CENTRE SPORTIF PFAFFENHOLZ

Basel

Herzog & de Meuron Architekten, AG 1992–93

body is a symptomatic expression caused by the increasingly virtual world around us ... but these trends, whether they appear to be polarised or chaotic, always have an inner coherence which is not obvious at first sight and that is what we are interested in. For us it is inspiring to collaborate with artists who concentrate on the treatment of surfaces. This collaboration has become a crucial factor in our design. Today, the individual house plays a very different role than in the past. The perception of architecture works via different channels of communication and the phenomenon of tattooing is applied as one possible way of communication, of mediation. But such an inscription also has a very direct impact on another level which endows the materials with a unique and new character. Tattoos, body building, piercing, aerobics, etc., are signs of the very strong present-day preoccupation with people's own bodies; this human need and desire to communicate with one's body within an alienated world, however, cannot be compared so directly to our use of images in order to generate new surfaces for spaces and entire building. Ultimately, our research focuses on questions such as: what is surface and what is space? How can it be captured, how can it be generated and how can it survive as a relevant subject in our contemporary culture?

ADDRESS St Louis, France
CLIENT Bürgerspital Basel
STRUCTURAL ENGINEER Ingenieurbüro Andreas Zachmann, Basel
COST SFR9.8 million
SIZE 5466 square metres
TRAM 3 to Burgfelden Grenze
ACCESS open

Herzog & de Meuron Architekten, AG 1992–93

Herzog & de Meuron Architekten, AG 1992–93

Tinguely Museum

After Jean Tinguely's death in 1991, the F Hoffmann–La Roche Foundation asked Mario Botta to design a museum for a large part of the artist's work. Tinguely, a sculptor and experimental artist, and Botta, along with the Foundation, formed a 'dream-team'. This constellation evoked criticism from those who felt that the confinement of Tinguely's work in a proper museum would contradict the artist's anti-institutional and playful intentions. They would rather have seen the 'machines délirantes' out on the street.

The site is bordered by the extraordinary void of the Rhine on the one side, a continuous flow of trucks and cars on the elevated motorway bridge at the back and the nineteenth-century Solitude Park at the front. The entire building is clad in natural red stone. An imposing solid wall functioning as a sound barrier is placed against the elevated motorway. The façade facing the park is almost entirely transparent and is interrupted only by the walls carrying the metal roof structure. Yet the museum's most dramatic feature is the fully glazed corridor that each visitor passes through before entering the exhibition spaces. Inside, Botta created relatively large and fairly neutral exhibition spaces following the conviction that the artist's work needed no preconceived rooms.

MH/TH What do you think about the phenomenon of the increasing polarisation into star-architecture or non-architecture?

Mario Botta You know this talk about star-architects always makes me laugh. I deny being a star-architect. It is an artificial label which is out of my reach. I became a star-architect with the houses I built 30 years ago. Back then I was sure not to be a star-architect, because I didn't even have enough to eat. It's bizarre, the consensus for architecture always arrives too late. You're already engulfed in new projects when

Basel

Mario Botta 1993–96

people come and want to talk about projects which were done 10 years ago. It's a social thing that doesn't touch me.

MH/TH But it's nonetheless a significant and increasing phenomenon of our culture ....

MB Yes, sure. ... I'll give you a general, a bit far-fetched, theory: ours is a world which is made only to be consumed: McDonald's, Coke. ... Those who manage to produce something creative in such a world get out of this dimension, but immediately become an image. So it's the consumer society which produces the stars, but it only appreciates their image. But the process goes on. I have many clients who approach me and only want the signature. I try to renounce this if I can. I am interested in addressing an architectural problem, not in creating an image. In a way it's quite sad, because they don't actually want your full capacity. It's a kind of a game.

ADDRESS Grenzacherstrasse 210A, 4002 Basel
CLIENT Hoffmann–La Roche AG, Basel
TECHNICAL ARCHITECTS GSG Baucontrol, Basel
STRUCTURAL ENGINEERING W G G Bauingenieure, Basel
SIZE 6057 square metres
TRAM 2 from Basel main station, then change at Wettsteinplatz for bus 31 to Solitude
WEBSITE www.tinguely.ch
ACCESS Wednesday to Sunday, 11.00–19.00

Mario Botta 1993–96

Tinguely Museum

Basel

Mario Botta 1993–96

Warteck Brewery

The renovation and extension of the former Warteck brewery, built between 1890 and 1935, gave Diener & Diener the chance to interpret a full city block by investigating its contemporary potentials and implications. The block is roughly divided into three parts: a new office building with an interior light well, and clad in green concrete slabs; a new residential complex in brick, built around a semi-enclosed courtyard; and a few buildings of the old factory devoted to cultural use.

Roger Diener describes the result as 'town planning that refuses to participate in a large or total order' and is consciously positioned between all prevailing categories, an attitude characteristic of the office's architecture. All new buildings are autonomous objects, subtly undermining the idea of the block perimeter development, but nevertheless engaging in what can be called a figurative constellation. Set back from existing building lines, the objects are understood as standing inside, and not at the edge, of the property. Their position and shape have the effect of visually closing the city block while, in fact, it is opened up.

The historic city block strictly differentiates between inside and outside, between public, semi-public and private. All such boundaries are dissolved in the Warteckareal, which allows the city's ground to run right up to the edge of the buildings. The entire open ground is in effect a large square, differentiated by the alteration of surface materials and the different dimensions characterising the spaces between buildings. The main circulation passage is as wide as the surrounding streets. It is through such operations that Diener & Diener achieves what is perceived as a stimulating uncertainty – to differentiate subtly without being prescriptive.

MH/TH Diener deliberately left the private or public use of the grounds largely undetermined. Is it up to the inhabitants to decide …?

Diener & Diener, Suter & Suter Planer, AG 1992–96

Diener & Diener, Suter & Suter Planer, AG 1992–96

Warteck Brewery

Martin Steinmann (architectural critic) Yes, but except for the ateliers there are neither direct exits leading to this ground, nor are there any balconies. There are few possibilities for an 'outward display' of private affairs. The ground always stays a collective space. This is different with the restaurant as a public locale, which puts its tables and chairs outside. But there are no boundaries between the different zones. I think that is an elemental feature for an urban condition.

MH/TH But this openness seems to get lost in the inner court of the apartment building, due to its restricted dimensions.

MS That is possible, but I think it is meant to have a different quality. It clearly belongs to the apartment house, while the other spaces are all in between buildings.

MH/TH But what purpose is it meant to serve? It is clearly designed to prevent anybody from using it.

MS Do you think that is wrong? This space creates distance. Contrary to prevailing sociologists' views, I think it is something marvellous to have green distancing spaces which discourages people to set up their deck chairs. Where do you find such spaces? It is neither a courtyard, nor a backyard. It doesn't fit in any category.

ADDRESS Grenzacherstrasse 62/64, Fischerweg 6/8/10, Alemannengasse 33/35/37, 4058 Basel
CLIENT Warteck Invest AG
STRUCTURAL ENGINEERING Suter & Suter AG; Cyrill Burger & Partner AG
SIZE 31,219 square metres
TRAM 2, 15 to Wettsteinplatz
ACCESS exterior open; interior by appointment only

Diener & Diener, Suter & Suter Planer, AG 1992–96

Diener & Diener, Suter & Suter Planer, AG 1992–96

Migros-Markt

MH/TH Can architecture influence the way we buy our groceries?

Roger Diener Not directly, but in a way, yes. Every building leaves traces in our memory, the result of experience, that will become the basis for new experiences ... for us and for the users.

MH/TH Markus Friedli [architect and critic] wrote that all parts of this building are aiming for an appropriate expression of 'public'. What characterises this small Migros as a public building?

RD It's possible that this building evokes associations with different kinds of public buildings, anything from a market hall to a drive-in shop. ... For us, however, it only becomes interesting once these various references are embedded within the very structure of the building, on a much subtler level than a mere application of images ....

MH/TH If there's one prominent characteristic of your architecture it is the careful analysis of the context. At the same time you have also designed a 'mail-order-house', the exact opposite really ....

RD It is the strategy resulting from the unknown conditions of a site which made the design interesting. The house is assembled of various volumes which define different exterior spaces. The many possibilities of treating the staggered façades considerably influence the house's expression. To establish the specific relationship with the surroundings is out of our reach ... and this is something we find very exciting!

ADDRESS Riehenstrasse 315, 4058 Basel
CLIENT Migros Genossenschaft, Basel
STRUCTURAL ENGINEER Walther, Mory, Maier Bauingenieure AG, Basel
SIZE 1644 square metres
TRAM 2, 6 to Eglisee
ACCESS open

Diener & Diener 1993–96

Diener & Diener 1993–96

Ackermätteli School

At first glance it seems that the school is yet another rigid and monotonous box; a second glance reveals that its seeming simplicity is in fact rather complex. The view of the school from the open meadow to the west gives the impression that it has two corners missing. The inner façade's rhythmically arranged window pattern does not stop in the corner but instead folds the windows, almost as if they are moulded on to the building's skeleton. The large, almost square windows are identical on all sides: framed with black-coloured concrete casements and set back, they underline the punched openings and the depth of the façades. All the elements create a tension that evades an all-too-easy label.

The volumetric arrangement of the L-shaped building extends the half-finished block perimeter structure, while retaining its solitary character. The four storeys contain classrooms of various sizes, a crèche, a school kitchen, a gym and an auditorium. All classrooms are aligned along the outer façade, while access corridors and stairways face the court. On each floor the extra-wide corridors open on to larger gathering spaces which function as school yards.

Ackermann & Friedli, based in Basel and Schaffhausen, are best-known for their school projects, of which Ackermätteli is the largest.

ADDRESS Rastatterstrasse 32, 4057 Basel
CLIENT Baudepartement Basel-Stadt
STRUCTURAL ENGINEERING Emch & Berger AG, Basel
COST SF9.74 million
SIZE 4053 square metres
TRAM 14 to Kleinhüningen
ACCESS school hours only: 9.00–17.00

Ackermann & Friedli 1995–96

Ackermann & Friedli 1995–96

Dreirosen-Klybeck School and housing

On a site dominated by heavy traffic, Morger & Degelo faced the difficult task of adding 29 apartments, classrooms and a large gymnasium to an older school that stood somewhat lost in the middle of a half-finished perimeter block complex. By redefining and consolidating the corners of the block, the architects reacted by not applying rigidly the obvious perimeter-block solution. The new additions transform the unfinished city block into a spiral-shaped development. Taking the historicist school as core, the development then follows the perimeter and gradually reduces its volumes until all that demarcates the boundary between inside and outside is a glazed portico. The bold step to recess the whole volume of the triple gymnasium into the ground created the possibility for a large school yard: inlaid glass blocks are the only indication of the enormous space below.

Artist Renée Levi was called on only after the design was finished. Nevertheless, her concept unified the inner courtyard. Using the fully glazed inner façade as a canvas, Levi 'painted' it in fresh colours: yellow curtains with blue, green and orange floral patterns are the simple means by which she brings blooming life into a stony environment.

ADDRESS Klybeckstrasse 111/113/115, 4057 Basel
CLIENT Baudepartement, Basel
STRUCTURAL ENGINEERING Jauslin & Stebler Ingenieure, Basel
COST SF20.2 million
SIZE 7873 square metres
TRAM 14, 17 to Dreirosenbrücke
ACCESS gym open only

Morger & Degelo 1993–97

Morger & Degelo 1993–97

Beyeler Museum

Hildy and Ernst Beyeler, Basel's best-known art dealers and collectors, own one of the most important private collections of modern masterpieces, as well as African and Oceanic artefacts. The Beyeler Foundation is the successful result of a close collaboration. Together, the client and the Italian architect Renzo Piano developed a programme in which the architectural aesthetics do not challenge the qualities of the art collection.

Piano's international fame goes back to another museum project, the Georges Pompidou cultural centre in Paris (1971–77). No other building of that time has stirred up as much emotion and heated argument as the Beaubourg. Twenty years on, Piano's projects still retain an original spirit devoted to the rationalisation and refinement of construction, while the fascination with solving and developing new methods of engineering and industrial design is always present. In this museum, most of the technical effort has gone into the control and optimisation of natural light. South-tilting glass louvres direct the natural light into a highly complex system of smaller operable louvres arranged in several layers. While the exhibitions are exposed to varying conditions of daylight, they are protected at the same time from too-intense direct lighting by the adjustable louvres in the roof structure. On the one hand, it is the complexity of the roof construction that brings Piano's architecture up to date with the latest technical achievements. Its filigree filling appears surprisingly light, so light, in fact, that it almost seems to float above the stone walls, as if the crisp, cantilevered canopy exerts no weight on the pillars. On the other hand, the red porphyry used for the exterior cladding gives the museum an archaic timelessness by changing its appearance according to the weather and lighting conditions.

The long porphyry street façade forms the backbone of the museum, which is laid out parallel along three 120-metre-long zones. The solid

Renzo Piano, Burckhardt & Partner 1997

Beyeler Museum

Basel

Renzo Piano, Burckhardt & Partner 1997

exterior is complemented by airy white walls on the interior; a clearly structured alignment of introverted spaces leads to the fully glazed end façades offering views of the pond and the lush green of Berower Park. Piano has created a serene and noble pavilion devoted to the quiet contemplation of the art within.

ADDRESS Basel Strasse 77, 4125 Riehen-Basel
CLIENT Fondation Beyeler, Basel
STRUCTURAL ENGINEERING Ove Arup International, London/
Cyrill Burger & Partner AG, Basel
COST SF55 million
SIZE 7000 square metres (exhibition 1900 square metres)
TRAM 6 to Riehen Dorf
WEBSITE www.beyeler.com
ACCESS daily, 10.00–18.00 (–19.00 in summer; –20.00 on Wednesdays)

Renzo Piano, Burckhardt & Partner 1997

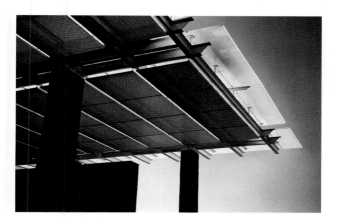

Basel

Renzo Piano, Burckhardt & Partner 1997

Greater Basel

Vitra, Weil am Rhein and Birsfelden

No architectural tourist visiting Switzerland or passing through Basel should miss the assembly of avant-garde architecture at Charles-Eames-Strasse 1–3 in Weil am Rhein, just across the Swiss–German border.

Vitra is a Swiss-owned manufacturer of designer furniture, but today it is almost better known for its architecture than for its chairs. Basel entrepreneur and collector Rolf Fehlbaum has established himself as Europe's foremost patron of architecture. When large parts of Vitra's factory in Weil burned down, Fehlbaum commissioned various internationally celebrated architects to design buildings for Vitra in Weil am Rhein in Germany and Birsfelden in Switzerland.

Comparing Vitra to an architectural theme park is inevitable. What started out as a small museum for Fehlbaum's private collection of chairs and a few new industrial buildings for his company has turned into a world-famous architectural Mecca attracting up to 40,000 tourists every year. The buildings refer to one another and yet develop their own theme. Owing to their close proximity, it is possible to get an appreciation of the work of these various architects in less than two hours. The patron's commitment to architecture seems to have a positive effect on the surroundings, the visitors and not least on the image projected by his company. The success of Vitra has made it the prime example of architecture in the service of contemporary 'corporate identity'.

MASTERPLAN AND FACTORY BUILDINGS
NICHOLAS GRIMSHAW 1981–87
After large parts of the Vitra factory in Weil were destroyed by fire in 1981, Fehlbaum invited the British architect Nicholas Grimshaw to masterplan the entire Vitra site. Known as a hi-tech expert, Grimshaw has built numerous industrial structures. The way he applies aluminium and steel

Grimshaw, Gehry, Hadid, Ando, Siza 1981–94

to his two factory buildings symbolises the technical know-how he is renowned for and the precision that Vitra guarantees in their products.

VITRA DESIGN MUSEUM
FRANK O GEHRY 1989

The meeting of Fehlbaum and the American architect Frank O Gehry, however, led to an abrupt reinterpretation of Vitra's planning concept. Gehry first came to Weil when his friends Claes Oldenburg and Coosje van Bruggen were installing their sculpture on site. Fehlbaum approached Gehry for a concept for a museum to house his growing furniture collection. It was Gehry's first realised project in Europe and his first all-white building. He openly admitted the formative effect that two architectural landmarks not far from here had on his design – Rudolf Steiner's Goetheanum II at Dornach (1925–28) and Le Corbusier's Chapel of Notre Dame at Ronchamps (1951–53). Gehry's highly expressive, if not expressionist, architecture results in a profusion of tilting towers, flaring façades and cantilevered canopies. The interior, on two floors around a inner centre, is an unexpectedly calm space, unlike the colliding forms of the exterior.

FIRE STATION
ZAHA M HADID 1993

Developing Zaha M Hadid's startling imagery of floating parallelograms from the first sketch to the finished building demanded an incredible architectural vision and commitment; not only Hadid and Fehlbaum, but also all engineers and workers were under great strains to turn the dynamic sketches into a three-dimensional reality. They managed to find a faithful conversion of the exploding plan, accompanied by a section

Grimshaw, Gehry, Hadid, Ando, Siza 1981–94

equally at odds with rectilinear norms. It was the first time that anyone had attempted to prove on such a large scale that Hadid's fleeting volumes and seemingly weightless planes could be translated into solid materials.

The building is not used as a fire station, but has been recycled as an extension of the Design Museum.

CONFERENCE CENTRE

TADAO ANDO 1993

Built in the same year as Hadid's fire station, the conference centre forms an antidote to the dramatic scenario of the fire station. Contrasting with Gehry's expressionist museum or Hadid's dynamically floating canopies, Tadao Ando serenely sinks his centre into the surrounding landscape. Instead of having a two-storey elevation above ground Ando decided to have a lower extension, subordinating his architecture to the orchard.

No other project on the site so emphasises the importance of nature. Barely noticeable imprints of three leaves in the wall of the concrete building pay respect to the three cherry trees that had to be felled for the centre. Ando has created a calm place for contemplation.

ASSEMBLY HALL

ALVARO SIZA 1993

Siza had to find a way to react to the growing complexity of the premises, building in the immediate proximity of works by Gehry, Grimshaw and Hadid. Siza was commissioned to design the largest factory building on the site, which he reduced to a few elements formulated in a hermetic brick-clad box. A clash of scale between the assembly hall and the much smaller fire station is avoided by Siza's calm proportions, which do not interfere with the fire station's sculptural qualities. The curved, trussed

Grimshaw, Gehry, Hadid, Ando, Siza 1981–94

Grimshaw, Gehry, Hadid, Ando, Siza 1981–94

canopy reaches out and links the assembly hall with Grimshaw's building. Functioning as a visual link between these two buildings, and as a frame for the fire station, part of the steel canopy can be lowered (from 11 to 4 metres above the ground) to protect the loading dock from rain.

VITRA CENTRE, BIRSFELDEN
FRANK O GEHRY 1994
Next to Vitra's original factory (1957), is the new Vitra Centre, the head office and communications centre. Situated amid a few modest business properties, Gehry's colourful expressionism is strongly set off. He contrasts the straightforward offices with the animated and multiform 'object villa'. Both buildings are connected with a large atrium, united under an imposing roof construction. Workplaces are in the office tract while the villa, with its sculptural forms, colours and lighting, provides the communicative focus. The many corners, edges and tensions are meant as a challenge to employees and visitors alike. Gehry's aim is to 'engage them, to get them angry and glad and thinking'.

ADDRESS Vitra Centre: Klünenfeldstrasse 22, 4127 Birsfelden;
Vitra Design Museum: Charles-Eames-Strasse 1–3, D-79574
Weil am Rhein, Germany
CAR E35 from Basel to Weil am Rhein
ACCESS museum open Tuesday to Friday, 14.00–18.00; Saturday, Sunday and public holidays, 11.00–17.00; guided tours (in English, German or French) are available by appointment – there is also a daily tour of the fire station and conference pavilion at 14.00; telephone +49 (0) 07621 70 3578
WEBSITE design-museum.de

Grimshaw, Gehry, Hadid, Ando, Siza 1981–94

Landscape Formation One, Weil am Rhein

Six years after the completion of her first building – the Vitra fire station (page 2.4) – Zaha Hadid returned to Weil am Rhein. The city of Weil commissioned the architect to design a pavilion for the national garden show Grün '99, for later use as a multifunctional exhibition space. Hadid, the only woman playing in the architectural major league, has long been receiving high critical acclaim, but has not had many opportunities to build her projects. She has finally been given the chance to realise several buildings, most notably the Contemporary Arts Center in Cincinnati and an arts centre in Rome.

The pursuit of the investigation into the relationship between ground and plan and the fluidity of spaces once again finds expression in Hadid's design for LF One. Interweaving inside and outside, bundles of lines emerge from and dissolve back into the landscape. The compressed mass gradually emerges and mutates into a boomerang-shaped ramp serving as a walking path, viewing platform and roof, all in one. The landscape is treated like architecture and the architecture like landscape. In the unexpected encounters of undulating vectors lies the tightly choreographed interplay of exhibition space, cafeteria, corridors and sinuous ramps.

CLIENT Stadtbauamt Weil-am-Rhein, Jürgen Hitze
STRUCTURAL ENGINEER Dr Ing L Martino, Grenzach-Wyhlen/Torino
COST DM3.4 million
SIZE 845 square metres
GETTING THERE follow the signs for Landesgartenschau
ACCESS exterior open; interior open during exhibitions

Zaha M Hadid 1996–99

Greater Basel

Zaha M Hadid 1996–99

Ricola-Europe, production and storage building

Our interest in the invisible world is in finding a form for it in the visible world. That is, in breaking through the deceptive, visible and familiar guise to take it apart, to atomise it, before relating to it anew. The invisible world is not a mystic one, but it is also not (only) a world of natural sciences, of invisible atomic crystalline structures. With this we mean the complexity of a system of relationships which exists in nature, in an un-researchable perfection, and whose analogy in the realm of art and society interests us. Our interest is thus the hidden geometry of nature, a spiritual principle and not primarily the outer appearance of nature.

Herzog & de Meuron, quoted in Peter Blum (ed.), *Architectures of Herzog & De Meuron*, Blumarts, Inc., New York, 1994

Herzog & de Meuron Architekten AG 1993

Ricola-Europe, production and storage building

Herzog & de Meuron Architekten AG 1993

Ricola-Europe, production and storage building

What I find important, what fascinates me is change, the fact that a building is always animated by different forms of appearance which make it responsive to its surroundings, to various kinds of perception. Architecture and also the fine arts show a kinship with this potential and this capacity for change-like the surface of water. (The surface of a body of water has an incredible variety of faces.) Depending on the weather and the light, it may seem entirely transparent or completely closed, guarded; it may seem as glass or it may have unique reflections. To me this variety which we call nature is absolutely captivating; mountains, the sky, or forests have this ability, too. And this variety is also a fascinating source of architectural expression.

Herzog & de Meuron, quoted in Peter Blum (ed.), *Architectures of Herzog & De Meuron*, Blumarts, Inc., New York, 1994

ADDRESS 1 rue del l'Ill, 68350 Mulhouse-Brunnstatt, France
CLIENT H P Richterich, chief executive of Ricola AG, Laufen
STRUCTURAL ENGINEER Andreas Zachmann, Basel
COST SF2.3 million
SIZE 2760 square metres
TRAM 18 from Mulhouse to 'Hirondelles'
CAR Dornach, Centre Universitaire, Brunstatt
ACCESS none; visible from the street

Herzog & de Meuron Architekten AG 1993

Ricola-Europe, production and storage building

Herzog & de Meuron Architekten AG 1993

Spittelhof housing, Biel-Benken

Peter Zumthor is often mistakenly believed to be a native of Grison. Actually he was born not far from Basel, where he has returned to build his first large housing project. In a hilly landscape on the northern edge of the Jura mountains, his housing complex sits on a ridge near the forest, overlooking the small village. Three loosely arranged units are inserted into the closely woven pattern of one-family houses. Two double-storey row houses follow the run of the ridge at different angles and create a trapezoidal inner space planted with gardens, meadows and trees. The three-storey apartment block, further up the hill, has a more urban character reflected in the organisation of the plan: all apartments have their own entrance accessed at ground level under a covered veranda – the most impressive space of the complex.

ADDRESS Spittelhofstrasse 1–11 and Am Rain 2–16, 4105 Biel-Benken
CLIENT Basellandschaftliche Beamtenversicherungskasse Liestal
STRUCTURAL ENGINEERING Engineering Partnership Affentranger & Müller, and Jürg Buchli
TRAIN from Basel, 17 to Oberwil or Therwil, then BLT BUS 64 to Biel-Benken
ACCESS open

Peter Zumthor 1989–96

Peter Zumthor 1989–96

Business School, Laufenburg

Located just outside the medieval town centre of Laufenburg, along the busy main street, the business school forms part of a new complex built on the site of former monastery gardens. The business school was completed in 1992, while the adjacent block of flats, also part of the competition for this site, was realised only in 1996 (page2.20).

A parallel arrangement of three parts comprising the school are distinguished by roof forms that give the building its characteristic contour. Even though every part is visible from the outside, such a differentiated reading is challenged by the material articulation of the façades. The red wood panels of the prominent main façade are extended to cover the side facing the large schoolyard, while green-tinted cement is used on the remaining two sides. This colour scheme, based on the complementary colours red and green, is used on the outside as well as in the interior.

A narrow, wedge-shaped entrance hall leads to a foyer and an elevated corridor, giving access to faculty rooms and classrooms. The north façade opens on to a small terrace sheltered from road noise and facing the block of flats recently completed by the same architects.

ADDRESS Winterthurerstrasse 3, 4335 Laufenburg
CLIENT Municipality of Laufenburg
STRUCTURAL ENGINEERING P Schmid, Hägglingen
TRAIN to Laufenburg, then a few minutes' walk
ACCESS school hours only: Monday to Friday, 9.00–17.00

Sumi & Burkhalter 1991–92

Sumi & Burkhalter 1991–92

Heimweg housing, Laufenburg

Part of a larger redevelopment plan in Laufenburg, this block is the second building by Sumi & Burkhalter, who built the nearby business school in 1992 (page 2.18). The concept was to create new living spaces for the many small families living in the medieval town centre. By offering them flats in the vicinity, space would be created for residences for larger families.

The block of flats lies on top of a ground-floor garage used by residents and the customers of the adjacent shopping centre. The basic structure consists of an exposed concrete plinth, prefabricated windows and panelling elements in a pattern repeated on each storey. On the upper floors flats are accessed from broad, terrace-like arcades dominated by protruding corbels which create rhythmic inlets of shadows and light. Colour gives cohesion and unity to the overall structure: dark grey for the panels, light blue for the undersides of the balconies, red and yellow for the porches. The broad arcades, which also function as semiprivate balconies, are the building's most characteristic feature. This inversion of the conventional anonymous arcade, which sacrifices a certain amount of privacy in favour of more communal living, encourages social interaction between the residents.

ADDRESS Heimweg 4, 4335 Laufenburg
CLIENT Wohnbaugenossenschaft Laufenburg
STRUCTURAL ENGINEERING Koch & Schmid, Laufenburg
COST SF3.8 million
SIZE 1148 square metres
TRAIN to Laufenburg, then a few minutes' walk
ACCESS none; visible from the street

Sumi & Burkhalter 1996

Greater Basel

Sumi & Burkhalter 1996

Zürich

Hauptbahnhof, extension platform roof

In 1847, the first railway in Switzerland linked Baden with the then prospering and quickly growing Zürich. It was largely due to the railway system that Zürich became the country's economic capital by the turn of the nineteenth century. Friedrich Wanner's main train station was inaugurated in 1871 and it still reflects the spirit of that age.

Just in time for the 150th anniversary of the Swiss Federal Railways in 1997, the last scaffolding came down marking the end of the seemingly never-ending succession of renovations and extensions to Zürich's main train station. In 1990, the subterranean concourse and shopping facilities opened, and in 1996 Ralph Bänzinger's controversial north wing was finally completed after many delays. That same year also saw the remaining temporary installations removed from the main hall, at last revealing this open space in its full grandeur.

The 250-metre-long platform roofs are the most recent addition. Instead of marking a clear boundary, the architects opened the station towards the city, creating a transitionary space characterised by the soaring dynamics of the new roof. Unlike the conventional roof that slopes down, protecting and embracing, this roof rises and exposes.

This most recent extension of Switzerland's busiest and most important train station, therefore, can be read as a sign of the *Zeitgeist* for the new millennium rather than merely as a functional improvement.

M Meili We were facing the problematic constellation of an urban situation which has undergone innumerable changes over the last 25 years. In this chaos it was crucial that whatever we decided to do had to be clear and minimal. Unlike the other competition projects we did not emphasise the transept: this axis no longer exists from an urban point of view. We therefore reduced the number of parts in the reading of the station

M Meili and M Peter, A Fickert and K Knapkiewicz 1996–97

Hauptbahnhof, extension platform roof

M Meili and M Peter, A Fickert and K Knapkiewicz 1996–97

Zürich

Hauptbahnhof, extension platform roof

from three to two: the main building and the tracks.

TH/MH Recent projects in Zürich have stirred up such heated discussions … everyone seems to have an opinion about it …

MM We have often been criticised for the autonomy of our intervention. … On the other hand, opting for a pleasing contextualism would have demanded the integration of all mistakes that had occurred over the years. … In the prevailing chaos we did not want to adapt and accommodate all aspects. We preferred to create a suborder justified by its relation to the whole.

TH/MH Especially on the Bahnhofstrasse-facing side, it is most obvious to observe the clash between two or more urban systems.

MM When dealing with such a huge thing as this station, collision inevitably becomes a fundamental compositional principle. Courage is necessary to let things collide. … The collision, however, is not a mere provocation but rather a wish to endow the urban node with sensibility. We knew we would not answer certain expectations and spatial conventions, but we are not making architecture in order to polemicise. Architecture has to remain positive in its essence and nothing is further from our aim than cynical commentary or mere entertainment.

ADDRESS Hauptbahnhof, 8001 Zürich
CLIENT Schweizerische Bundesbahnen
STRUCTURAL ENGINEERING Ing. Dr Lüchinger Partner AG (Dani Meier), Zürich
TRAIN to Hauptbahnhof
COST SF12 million
SIZE 9000 square metres
ACCESS 5.00–1.30

M Meili and M Peter, A Fickert and K Knapkiewicz 1996–97

Hauptbahnhof, extension platform roof

M Meili and M Peter, A Fickert and K Knapkiewicz 1996–97

Office building, Löwenplatz

In the late 1980s and 1990s, when few large projects were actually real-ised in Zürich, Theo Hotz – then already in his sixties – was one of the small number of architects able to build extensively in the inner city.

After the highly acclaimed Telecommunications Centre in Zürich-Herdern of the late 1970s, more commissions for large office buildings followed: the Marti Office Building, Thurgauerstrasse 56 (1985); the Apollo Office Building, Stauffacherstrasse 41 (1991); the Grünenhof Conference Centre, Nüschelerstrasse 2 (1991); the Feldpausch, Bahnhof-strasse 88 (1994); the Toro Office Building, Eduard-Imhof-Strasse (1997); and, most recently, the extension of the Department of Dentistry at Zürich University on Plattenstrasse (1998).

The office building on the Löwenplatz is a typical example of the archi-tect's quest for technical innovations and compositional clarity. State-of-the-art engineering and a plentiful use of glass and steel make his projects easy to spot in the stony cityscape. The curved glass container, with its two-storey retail storefront and double-layered skin, addresses its prom-inent position on a busy square; its volume appearing as if all planes and corners have been meticulously chiselled away to fit the building into the intricate street pattern.

ADDRESS Löwenplatz, 8001 Zürich
CLIENT Mathis AG
STRUCTURAL ENGINEERING Ing. Gasser & Scepan, Baar
COST SFr11 million
SIZE 1600 square metres
TRAM 3, 14, 10 to Löwenplatz
ACCESS store only, 9.00–18.30

Theo Hotz 1991–92

Office building, Löwenplatz

Zürich

Theo Hotz 1991–92

Telecab 200'0

Even owners of mobile phones should venture into a Telecab 200'0 just to experience the new age of telephone booths. As the heavy glass door slides smoothly to the side, a few seconds of spherical music resounds. Every detail of the booth is custom-designed and it looks expensive.

A new means of communication was the theme for this prototype, which was commissioned by a major billboard advertising company. The decision was made to discard the old, all-enclosed box in favour of a transparent cylinder, despite the loss of advertising space. Only one continuously illuminated poster adorns the new cabin. Although the 360-degree exposure in the new booth makes it less attractive for couples wanting to share a romantic moment, it also discourages people from using it as a toilet or committing acts of vandalism – all major concerns of the client. Numerous compliancy tests of the Federal Bureau of Material Standards, performed under the severest conditions, prove this phone booth able to withstand a hurricane, making it one of the safest spots in town.

As night falls, the brightly lit glass cylinders become points of reference and the semi-transparent top, which usually escapes notice during the day, takes on a life of its own: its lights radiate far into the darkness, changing colours at the stroke of midnight.

ADDRESS throughout Zürich and other cities
CLIENT APG-Schweiz and Swisscom
STRUCTURAL ENGINEERING Ing. Lips MSM AG
COST SF50,000 each
SIZE 1.5 square metres
ACCESS open

Hans Ulrich Imesch 1995

Telecab 200'0

Zürich

Hans Ulrich Imesch 1995

Issey Miyake boutique

Originally, there were two Issey Miyake boutiques in Zürich designed by Isa Stürm and Urs Wolf, but only this more recent one remains. Good interior design is still a rarity in Switzerland, where ingenious spatial concepts for boutiques have been largely neglected in favour of maximising the space for the display of goods. Quite tellingly, it is one of contemporary Japan's most important fashion designers who bestowed on Zürich the impulse for these creatively designed sales spaces.

Miyake's garments, with their strong, sculptural inflections, are displayed in the pure and imaginary space. The curved walls resemble a spiralling seashell, while the wooden cladding, low ceiling and procession to the lower store level, connected by a curved flight of steps, give the visitor a feeling of entering an organic form. Fluorescent lighting is installed in the sweeping partition and overflows on to the smooth wood panels, making them appear to glow. At night, this most prominent architectural component takes full possession of the space when all display panels are drawn in and the dimmed light fills the room.

ADDRESS Storchengasse 7, 8001 Zürich
CLIENT Erica Ouie AG, Zürich
COST SF450,000
SIZE 160 square metres
ACCESS Monday to Friday, 10.00–18.30; Saturday, 10.00–16.00

Isa Stürm and Urs Wolf 1991

Isa Stürm and Urs Wolf 1991

Hotel Widder

When an entire block of 23 houses in Zürich's historic old town was sold, it was obvious that only a powerful client could afford such an investment. Many of the houses dated from the Middle Ages and had been put under historical protection. When the decision was made to turn eight of the houses into a five-star hotel, it was clear that the project would take years to be realised ... and it did. Nine years and an estimated SF100 million later, the Hotel Widder opened its doors, offering guests a historical mosaic of the past millennium of the city.

The Widder is an easy project to criticise. Opulence and a superabundance of impressions and materials, easily imaginable in the booming 1980s, make one rather uncomfortable today. Lavish amounts of money spent on details might be expected for a first-class hotel, but probably less might actually have been more. Whatever one's thoughts on the renovation, Tilla Theus deserves respect for the courage and energy needed to take on such a project. She constantly devised new strategies and custom-made solutions to meet all possible (and impossible) demands. Not one detail escaped her attention and the architect's hand is seen and felt everywhere – a *tour-de-force* in every respect.

ADDRESS Widder Hotel, Rennweg 7, 8001 Zürich
CLIENT UBS, Zürich
STRUCTURAL ENGINEERING ACS-Partner AG, Zürich
COST SF100 million
TRAM 6, 7, 11, 13 to Rennweg/Augustinergasse
ACCESS restaurants, bars and library open

Tilla Theus & Partner, AG 1992–95

Zürich

Tilla Theus & Partner, AG 1992–95

Selnau housing complex

Formerly the site of Selnau train station, the city took the chance to create new living spaces in an area that has increasingly been dominated by commercial spaces and heavy through-traffic. Sixty apartments, offices and public spaces were created on this narrow, elongated site that borders a part of town that was planned on an orthogonal grid in the nineteenth century. Block perimeter buildings prevail, but it was impossible to treat all sides equally in view of the difficult urban context.

It is the straightforward design and refined composition of the 250-metre-long river-façade that demarcates a strong and convincing urban boundary. The ramp of the train tunnel underneath is articulated as a base of the building and serves as an elevated foot and bike path. The façade away from the river reflects the proportions of the neighbouring buildings and is only three stories high, which helps to bring in more sunlight to the inner courts – a welcome gesture in urban housing blocks.

Martin Spühler's wedge-shaped building is considerate in its connection to and extension of the existing urban structure, reacting to all three sides in different manners. It succeeds in transforming a fragmented corner to a real urban space.

ADDRESS Selnaustrasse 17, 8002 Zürich
CLIENT City of Zürich
STRUCTURAL ENGINEERING Meyer–Kaufmann–Snozzi, Zürich
COST SF55 million
SIZE 16,600 square metres
TRAIN S4, S10 to Bahnhof Selnau
TRAM 8 to Bahnhof Selnau
ACCESS public courtyards only

Martin Spühler 1992–95

Zürich

Martin Spühler 1992–95

Waschanstalt Zürich

The 30-metre-high chimney of the Waschanstalt is easy to spot. The clearly visible landmark bears witness to the building's more than a century-long history as a laundry. Until it closed in 1997, the Waschanstalt remained the last operating industrial site in Zürich situated directly on the lake. Not much remains of the old factory besides its chimney, the filter tower and the brick façade of the old office building.

The clear organisation into two long volumes creates a dense development while its proportions still refer to the factory's original scale. The internal alley divides the complex into a lake-oriented living and a street-facing office zone, dominated by three dark cantilevered boxes floating above the ground. A wide gravel strip connects the street with the harbour. This minimalist landscape strip, with its long concrete containers, separates the Waschanstalt from the adjacent public swimming area. The cool chic of the few chosen materials sets the tone for the entire complex. High ceilings, open-plan unrestricted views, perfect detailing and an unbeatable location are the very features that appeal to a young, upscale urban clientele.

ADDRESS Seestrasse 457–67, 8038 Zürich
CLIENT Wollimob AG, Zürich
STRUCTURAL ENGINEER APT Andreas Lutz, Zürich
LANDSCAPE ARCHITECTS Arge Ganz/Kuhn & Truninger
SIZE 7457 square metres
BUS 161 to Waschanstalt, Wollishofen
ACCESS outside only

Angélil/Graham/Pfenninger/Scholl Architecture 1999–2000

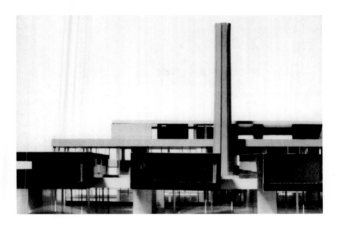

Zürich

Angélil/Graham/Pfenninger/Scholl Architecture 1999–2000

Brahmshof

In 1986, the Protestant Women's Association of Zürich held a competition with the intention to set an example for communal living. The ambitious brief specified 70 flats for the socially and economically marginalised: that is, for single-parent households, elderly people, students, as well as for the mentally and physically handicapped who were shown to be most likely to be in difficult living conditions. A café, offices, artist ateliers, a nursing school, crèches and common rooms were also to be incorporated.

Kuhn Fischer Partners won the competition with their proposal for a large perimeter block along the Brahmsstrasse, adding three volumes to an already existing L-shaped children's home to create an inward-oriented block with two courtyards. On the ground floor are public and semipublic spaces, while housing occupies the three upper levels. The floor plan of the flats is flexible, and individual rooms can be enlarged or detached as necessary.

A system of detached corridors on all levels accesses the apartments facing the inner court. These outdoor corridors create a communal space blurring the boundary between the private balconies and the public corridor.

ADDRESS Brahmsstrasse 22–24, 8003 Zürich
CLIENT Evangelischer Frauenbund, Zürich
STRUCTURAL ENGINEER Ing. Jean-Paul Jäger AG, Adliswil
COST SF1.67 million
SIZE 10,144 square metres
TRAM 2, 3 to Albisriederplatz
ACCESS courtyard and café only

Kuhn Fischer Partners 1989–91

Kuhn Fischer Partners 1989–91

Stadelhofen station, renovation and extension

Every four minutes a train arrives at Stadelhofen station and pours commuters into the city. Stadelhofen used to be a minor stop on a suburban line, but today it is a vital link in the city's infrastructure where trains, trams and the Forchbahn, another regional railway line, converge.

With its opening in 1990, the renovation and extension of the station immediately became one of Zürich's most intrinsic landmarks. It is often forgotten that this winning competition entry that unmistakably carries Santiago Calatrava's signature was actually the result of a collaboration with Arnold Amsler and Werner Rüeger. This expressive structure, which is unlike any other building in Zürich, was positively received by the people of the city. The Swiss preference for box-like, rectilinear construction was fundamentally challenged by the Spanish architect's vision of strangely zoomorphic forms. The flow of energy, the poised masses and the momentary balance achieved by the bone-like structure of spiky beams give the station a prehistoric as well as a futuristic feeling. The construction of concrete, steel and glass resembles a huge, partially excavated skeleton whose bones emerge from the hill, follow its outline and disappear again in the ground.

The station is organised on three levels: above the tracks lies a promenade that will eventually be overgrown with plants to form a green canopy cascading over the walls; on the ground level is a 270-metre-long platform consisting of repeated, tripartite, Y-shaped columns that support either glass or concrete canopies; and one level below, the commercial level that links the tracks exploits the sculptural qualities of concrete and resembles a huge ribcage. All of this is centred on the pedestrians who permeate the station at all levels through the multifold connections – lifts, escalators, stairs, bridges. The organisation of train arrivals and depar-

Santiago Calatrava, Arnold Amsler, Werner Rüeger 1983–90

Stadelhofen station, renovation and extension

Santiago Calatrava, Arnold Amsler, Werner Rüeger 1983–90

Stadelhofen station, renovation and extension

tures shows how well this station functions. Most trains coming from the outskirts of Zürich arrive on platform 1, which gives the masses of hurried commuters immediate access to the city. In the evening most outward-bound trains leave from platforms reached by the subterranean concourse, so that commuters can do their shopping before going home.

The juxtaposition of the historical construction with Calatrava's futuristic steel and concrete construction works well. Neither dominates the other, as the old building's main façade overlooking the square remains the focal point for people coming from the city, and the new intervention lies hidden behind the densely built house fronts. As soon as this dramatic and most unusual construction comes into sight, however, it exerts a mesmerising force. The eye-catching detailing of the steel joints and soaring beams, and the immense masses of concrete that seem miraculously suspended in mid-air keep visitors in awe of Calatrava's engineering capabilities and architectural vision. In addition, Stadelhofen must be recognised as Zürich's most successful urban intervention of the last decade.

ADDRESS Stadelhoferplatz, 8001 Zürich
CLIENT SBB
STRUCTURAL ENGINEERING Dr Santiago Calatrava, Zürich
TRAIN S2, S5, S6, S9 (one stop from main station)
TRAM 11, 15 to Stadelhofen, 2, 4 to Opernhaus
ACCESS shopping concourse during railway opening hours

Santiago Calatrava, Arnold Amsler, Werner Rüeger 1983–90

Zürich

Santiago Calatrava, Arnold Amsler, Werner Rüeger 1983–90

Mühlebachstrasse, renovation

In the immediate vicinity of the Stadelhofen train station is Franz Romero and Markus Schaefle's renovation and conversion of two residential buildings into offices. This project is a successful example that does not destroy – but actually strengthens and adds to – the old structure.

Over time the two original buildings underwent several changes and were eventually merged. The most recent renovation completely replaced the cluttered courtyard façade with a new transparent skin of steel, wood and glass. A grid of one-storey-high windows in box-like frames now extends over the entire façade. The architects have transformed an anonymous 1920s' building into a functional, light-flooded structure adapted to contemporary office requirements.

The office's sensibility for material and detail is apparent on the new back façade. On the street façade the architects' intervention was basically reduced to a cleansing of later additions and the recovery of the original structure.

The fruitful collaboration with landscape architects Kienast Vogt Partners enlivened the site with an unconventional front and back garden. The garden was only possible due to the reduction of the assigned parking from nine to only three spaces.

ADDRESS Mühlebachstrasse 11, 8032 Zürich
CLIENT Basler & Partner Ing.
COST SF300,000
TRAM 2, 4, 11, 15 to Stadelhofen
ACCESS none; visible from the street

Romero & Schaefle/Kienast & Vogt 1997

Mühlebachstrasse, renovation

Romero & Schaefle/Kienast & Vogt 1997

ZELO hair salon

After being over-exposed to hair-raising architecture on your trip through Switzerland, why not treat yourself to a snazzy new look in a stylish environment? On Seefeldstrasse, amid stone façades in various shades of grey, the bright colours of ZELO stand out. Instead of a cool company logo, the colour-permeated room acts as an advertisement for the hair salon. At night, when the empty space remains fully lit, it radiates colour into the darkness and takes on a strangely surreal quality. It is difficult to get a sense of the actual space, which seems divided only into surfaces and colours. The resulting impression of two-dimensionality recalls the hyper-reality of computer-rendered images.

ADDRESS Seefeldstrasse 182, 8008 Zürich
CLIENT Fabio Schmid Productions
COST SF250,000
SIZE 90 square metres
TRAM 2, 4 to Fröhlichstrasse
ACCESS Thursday and Friday, 9.00–18.30; Saturday, 9.00–16.00

Jasmin Grego and Joseph Smolenicky 1992

ZELO hair salon

Zürich

Jasmin Grego and Joseph Smolenicky 1992

Hotel Zürichberg, renovation and extension

Hotel Zürichberg was founded in 1899 by the Zürich Women's Association for Alcohol-free Restaurants (ZFV). The idea of a hotel reflecting the society's aim of a healthy lifestyle governed by light, air and sunshine seemed unrealistic, but the building was realised against all odds. It became popular, even though it had to compete with the glamorous Grand Hotel Dolder nearby. Built around the same time in the Swiss chalet style of the late nineteenth century, the Dolder attracted a chic, indulgent, international clientele fond of the more extravagant pleasures money can buy. (It still does.) The Zürichberg has remained a favourite spot for a leisurely promenade on a sunny afternoon.

For its centenary, the ZFV commissioned the renovation and extension of the Zürichberg. The Commission for Monuments' Preservation decided, retrospectively, to give certain parts of the main building historic status. Sumi & Burkhalter's winning project was thus totally changed as they were required to redress the primary problem of providing parking space for 70 cars and an additional 30 bedrooms.

The result is a detached annex with neither back, front nor entrance, accessed solely through a subterranean corridor connecting the main building to the new wing. The corridor's dark wooden parquet and rusty red painted walls are dimly lit by a soft blue light. A slight bend in the corridor prevents the visitor from having a full view of the annex from afar. There is a moment of surprise on entering the airy atrium and following the slow-rising elliptical ramp, the main motif of the annex. (The ramp is extended by the three-storey underground garage 'screwed' into the ground.) This space inescapably evokes associations with its bigger sibling – the Guggenheim Museum by Frank Lloyd Wright in New York. The hotel rooms are plain but tastefully furnished, with movable

Sumi & Burkhalter 1993–95

Sumi & Burkhalter 1993–95

units that transform the bedroom effortlessly into an office. Each room has a balcony with a wooden sliding screen and a bathroom with natural lighting. The isolation, low elevation and wood sheathing of the façade separate the annex from the more prominent main building, giving it the appearance of a pavilion in a clearing.

Even for those who cannot spend the night, this hotel is definitely worth the trip. On a sunny day, one can enjoy a cup of coffee or a glass of non-alcoholic beer on the terrace overlooking the lake and mountains.

ADDRESS Orellistrasse 21, 8044 Zürich
CLIENT ZFV
STRUCTURAL ENGINEERING J Spahn, Zürich
COST SF24 million
TRAM 6 to Zürich Zoo
ACCESS open

Sumi & Burkhalter 1993–95

Sumi & Burkhalter 1993–95

Zoo entrance and restaurant

In accordance with surrounding residential zoning requirements, the zoo was originally organised in parcels of land along a main axis – a precautionary measure should the zoo prove economically unprofitable. A new zoo concept seeks to abolish these old structures to create a didactic journey taking the visitor through cageless displays that are simulations of the animals' original habitats. This approach supports the trend in zoos as lively, interactive and popular resorts rather than as animal sanctuaries.

The zoo is already Zürich's most visited institution, attracting masses of people at the weekend. A first phase of restructuring and expansion therefore concentrates on a new entrance zone, so ensuring the easy handling of visitors. The competition was won by local architects Jean-Pierre Dürig and Philippe Rämi who have been acclaimed for winning competition projects in Switzerland and abroad: most notably, their first prize for the extension to the Prado in Madrid and third prize in the Yokohama Pier competition.

The white exterior wall swings around the curving street, making a barrier and contrasting starkly with the adjoining residential area through its organic forms. The architects' arrangement of horizontal and vertical planes results in an easy and relaxed progression of spaces.

ADDRESS Zürichbergstrasse 221, 8004 Zürich
CLIENT Zoo Zürich
COST SF13 million
SIZE 2755 square metres
TRAM 5, 6 to Zoo
ACCESS summer 8.00–18.00; winter 9.00–17.00

Jean-Pierre Dürig and Philippe Rämi 1998–99

Zürich

Jean-Pierre Dürig and Philippe Rämi 1998–99

Riff-Raff Cinema and Bar

This small cinema with its trendy bar is just a few steps off Langstrasse, Zürich's notorious red-light district. Riff-Raff attracts the young audience frequenting the 'off-culture' shops, bars and restaurants that have been established recently in this part of town. This lively neighbourhood offers a welcome alternative to the world-famous bbourgeois Bahnhofstrasse which is dominated by suits and fur coats.

The locale in the Neugasse has recently been taken over by a cooperative promoting independent cinema productions. Nowadays, when audiences are increasingly confronted with mega-cinema complexes, Riff-Raff appears exotic. Two small auditoria are separated by the bar, which is the heart of the movie-theatre.

The elegant bar, using prune furnice, evokes images of a yacht with luxurious mahogany-clad interiors. It functions as the primary lightsource in an otherwise dimly lit space. The primary feature is the projection beam cutting across the room above the heads of the lounging crowd. To the horror of anti-tobacco lobbyists, smoking is welcome because it enhances the effects of the light sculpture created by the projection beam. Patrons are reviving the building's history which dates back to the beginning of the twentieth century when it showed silent films.

ADDRESS Neugasse/Langstrasse, 8005 Zürich
CLIENT Neugass Kino AG, Zürich
STRUCTURAL ENGINEERING Ing. Reto Bonomo, Rüdlingen
COST SF2.1 million (including technical equipment)
SIZE 440 square metres
TRAM 4, 13 to Limmatplatz
BUS 32 to Röntgenstrasse
ACCESS cinema 14.00–00.30; bar open

M Meili, M Peter and A Staufer, Th Hasler Architekten 1997–98

Zürich

M Meili, M Peter and A Staufer, Th Hasler Architekten 1997–98

SVA

The dramatic z-shaped building is a fresh breeze in Zürich's contemporary architectural landscape. Wedged in between the railway tracks and early twentieth-century apartment buildings, the eye-catching sculptural volume is a landmark. The adjoining brightly coloured apartment cubes were also part of the competition won by Isa Stürm and Urs Wolf in 1990. It is Zürich's first large project by a younger generation of architects.

The building's nine façades offer changing and very different perspectives. The razor-sharp cantilevered edge points towards Langstrasse. The long façade parallel to Röntgenstrasse is dominated by the slightly protruding seamless glass bands wrapping themselves around every corner and differentiated multilevelled façades open towards the cubes.

The alternation of glass and limestone sets the rhythm, stressing the pronounced horizontal bands, and creating the illusion that the stony layers rest on glass only. This gains even larger prominence when lit at night, as the glow of the green glass layers radiates a cool light.

A change of client meant that the architects were left in charge of only the office building, leaving the realisation of the apartment blocks to a commercial entrepreneur. Unfortunately, all that is left of the apartments' original design is the outer shell and the concept for the outside space.

ADDRESS Röntgenstrasse 17, 8005 Zürich
CLIENT SVA Zürich
STRUCTURAL ENGINEER Walt & Galmarini, Zürich
LANDSCAPE ARCHITECT Rotzler Krebs Partner, Winterthur
COST SF55 million
SIZE 18,000 square metres
BUS 32 to Röntgenstrasse
ACCESS exterior and lobby

Isa Stürm and Urs Wolf 1990–99

Isa Stürm and Urs Wolf 1990–99

Löwenbräu Areal and Kunsthalle

The Löwenbräu complex – originally a brewery from the 1950s – has been recycled to house two museums, several galleries, a bookshop and a fitness centre. Just around the corner from the Steinfels complex (page 3.40), this is another addition to a neighbourhood that is currently the hippest part of town. With the onset of the de-industrialisation in the late 1970s, accelerated by recession in the 1990s, many former industrial sites have been re-appropriated: initially taken over by the off-culture, they are increasingly replaced by trendy upscale locales.

The Committee for Historical Monuments explicitly required the preservation of the factory's character. Most of the work was done by Christian Karrer and Andreas Fuhrimann who designed the exhibition spaces for the Kunsthalle in the former bottling plant, while the packing area was converted by Andreas Marazzi into the Museum of Contemporary Art. Together, they have created some of the most interesting art spaces in Zürich and, in combination with the galleries, the factory has become the new hot spot for art lovers. Today, the Löwenbräu provides numerous, generous and unpretentious spaces for multipurpose uses. The indeterminate character of the architecture generates a refreshing atmosphere, leaving open the possibilities for future uses.

ADDRESS Limmatstrasse 270, 8005 Zürich
TRAM 4, 13 to Escher-Wyss
ACCESS Tuesday to Friday, 12.00–18.00; Saturday and Sunday, 11.00–17.00

Andreas Fuhrimann and Christian Karrer/Andreas Marazzi 1995–96

Andreas Fuhrimann and Christian Karrer/Andreas Marazzi 1995–96

Steinfels

The Steinfels complex is one of many industrial sites that in recent years had to close production and look for new users. In a first phase, architects Kaufmann and van der Meer restructured the two factory buildings that form the core of the complex. They are now home to new users such as a cinema, a game parlour, a dance school, a restaurant, a television station and 49 apartments. The architects replaced the dilapidated parts of the old factory with a new construction containing three luxurious lofts, apartments and some ateliers. Traditional industrial building materials were avoided in favour of modern prefabricated elements of aluminium, wood or concrete. Corrugated aluminium panels, brightly coloured wood boards and very large windows structure the façades and accentuate the difference between old and new. This juxtaposition is further emphasised by the interior corridor demarcating the structural boundary.

While the two large factory buildings have already been renovated and handed over to their new tenants, all other subsidiary buildings were temporarily used by people who worked and lived there. This heterogeneous mix gave the whole city an air of living-friendly urbanity quite unlike any other in Zürich. This stimulating period of transition came to an abrupt end in January 2000 when the subsidiary buildings were torn down to make room for the next building phase.

ADDRESS Heinrichstrasse 267, 8005 Zürich
CLIENT Steinfels AG
STRUCTURAL ENGINEER Dr Hr Schalcher
COST SF38.8 million
SIZE 13,500 square metres
TRAIN Hardbrücke; TRAM Escher-Wyss-Platz
ACCESS none; visible from the street

Kaufmann, van der Meer & Partner 1993–95

Steinfels

Kaufmann, van der Meer & Partner 1993–95

Zürich

IBM Headquarters

IBM's move from the central General Guisan Quai to Zürich-Altstetten confirms the trend for corporations to shift their headquarters from city centres to the periphery. Elegant yet restrained proportions and use of materials give the new headquarters a distinguished appearance.

The large cuboid volume marks a strong urban presence in a hitherto largely undefined part of town. Twenty-five-metre-high towers at the corners characterise the street façade. The glass and aluminium window frames subtly contrast with the grey granite cladding.

The square volume (64 by 79 metres) with its relatively low 19-metre elevation has a stout, solid character and is oriented inwards around a courtyard. In an area dominated by inhospitable industrial complexes, this inner court creates a welcoming public meeting space. The ground floor of the stepped central space serves as an open-air café.

The Ticino architects Campi & Pessina are best known for their monochromatic white villas of the 1970s and 1980s indebted to Italian and American modernism. The IBM headquarters and the new building for the Chemistry Department of the ETH Zürich (page 3.44) are the office's first major projects north of the San Gotthard Pass.

ADDRESS Beandliweg 21, 8048 Zürich
CLIENT IBM Schweiz
STRUCTURAL ENGINEERING Henauer Engineers, Zürich
COST SF100 million
SIZE 27,100 square metres
TRAIN S-Bahn to Bahnhof Altstetten
ACCESS by appointment only

Mario Campi & Franco Pessina 1992–96

Zürich

Mario Campi & Franco Pessina 1992–96

ETH Hönggerberg, extension

Since the 1950s, increasingly tight space at the ETH (Federal Institute of Technology) has begged an expansion. Architect Albert H Steiner designed the first phase: infrastructure and the Physics and Biology departments (1966–73); while Max Ziegler and Erik Lanter did the extension for Architecture and Building Sciences (1972–76). The most recent extension by Mario Campi & Franco Pessina is still under construction.

This latest extension of the campus is the biggest federal construction site in Switzerland of the late 1990s. It adds an additional 58,000 square metres, increasing the usable space by 50 per cent. It is comprised of three parts: a comb-shaped volume with teaching and research facilities for the physics, chemistry, biology and material science departments, an attached auditorium building, and a separate service building.

The architects emphasise a more tightly knit unity of the various buildings by creating a piazza and redirecting the main access road for public transportation. Economical use of land and functional aspects dictate the formal expression, imposing order and rhythm through geometry, repetition and formal simplicity. No doubt, infrastructural efficiency, excellent organisation and high ecological standards are guaranteed on all levels, but a more daring vision would perhaps be better suited to an architecture bridging the twentieth and the twenty-first centuries.

ADDRESS Albert Einsteinstrasse, 8093 Zürich
CLIENT Amt für Bundesbauten
LANDSCAPE ARCHITECTS Kienast Vogt Partners, Zürich
COST about SF30 million (first phase)
SIZE 58,000 square metres (first phase)
BUS 69 to ETH Hönggerberg
ACCESS interior open during office hours

Mario Campi & Franco Pessina 1997–2004

Zürich

Mario Campi & Franco Pessina 1997–2004

Toro I

At first glance, this office for Asea Brown Bovery is not spectacular, but the five-storey building was completed to budget, and three months ahead of schedule in the amazingly short time (for Switzerland) of two years.

Traditionally, architects in Switzerland not only design, but also make the working drawings, supervise construction, measure quantities, estimate costs, and are often the main contractor. This allows for rigorous control over construction, and together with good craftsmanship it tends to result in the quality and precision cherished and unique to the country.

With Toro I, as well as other recent buildings, Theo Hotz shows how to achieve this quality and precision while collaborating with major general contractors such as Oerlikon-Bührle, AG and powerful clients like ABB Switzerland. Hotz works within precisely those constellations that many of his colleagues believe to be evil forces undermining their profession. His office operates with an admirable professionalism, demonstrated in an understanding of the design implications on cost and building management, neither losing grip on the overall design nor the 1:1 detail. Hotz has redefined the profession by producing work that is neither revolutionary nor anonymous, but rather exceptionally good. He thus occupies an important place in a culture increasingly polarised between star- and non-architecture.

ADDRESS Brown Boveri-Strasse, 8050 Zürich
CLIENT ABB Daimler Benz Transportation, AG
COST SF90 million
SIZE 22,800 square metres
TRAIN S-Bahn to Oerlikon
BUS 80 direction Affoltern
ACCESS none; visible from the street

Theo Hotz 1995–97

Toro I

Zürich

Theo Hotz 1995–97

Greater Zürich

Kunstmuseum extension, Winterthur

The neo-classical Kunstmuseum, which has an important collection of modern art, has long been in need of more exhibition space. In choosing an industrial architecture type using prefabricated materials, Annette Gigon and Mike Guyer have given their extension its own character and met the client's requirement for an economic and temporary structure.

Their concept of 'nine spaces, some windows' finds a balance between adding a clearly defined autonomous structure and maintaining a dialogue with the main building. The only structural link between the two buildings, a elevated footbridge clad in steel, mediates between the stone façade of the old building and the glass of the new extension. The stark contrast between the classicist art temple and the industrial building is very strong, provoking associations with the city's own history as one of Switzerland's foremost turn-of-the-century industrial centres.

The architects' solution is a simple glass box sustained by a steel frame. The exhibition space rests on pilotis above the car park, thereby maintaining the requirement for the retention of public parking. The simplicity and compactness of the building's outer appearance is also reflected in its internal organisation.

The access corridor on the first floor is hidden at the back of the main building and leads down a stairs into the new tract. Nine rooms are symmetrically arranged in a rectangular floorplan. There are meandering passages with no prescribed route for the visitor who experiences the resistance and reopening of the spaces. The simple cast-concrete floor and white plastered walls are evenly lit by the shed roof extending over the building. Three huge windows extending from floor to ceiling endow the rooms with a unique character. Their size and the views they frame are, at times, even more breathtaking than the works exhibited. It makes the windows the most spectacular element in the otherwise very reduced and

Annette Gigon & Mike Guyer 1995

Annette Gigon & Mike Guyer 1995

straightforward exhibition space.

The quality of the prefabricated profiled glass strips as used from top to bottom shows the architects' ingenuity in dealing with the creative possibilities offered by apparently plain industrial materials. The glass sheathes the building's structure like a shimmering and subtly luminescent green veil. The profiles on the ground floor form the walls, allowing light to enter during the day while shining out from inside at night. On the upper level, however, these same profiles are impermeable to light and they function only as protection of the insulation.

The solidity of the neo-classical stone building is confronted with the lightness of a glass box supported by seemingly even more delicate, thin glass pilasters. This fragility and transparency underlines the ephemerality of the extension as it perches lightly on the site.

ADDRESS Museumstrasse 52, 8400 Winterthur; tel.: 052 267 51 62
CLIENT Kunstverein Winterthur
STRUCTURAL ENGINEERING Branger & Conzett, Chur
COST SF4 million
SIZE 1000 square metres (without parking)
TRAIN to Winterthur then a 5-minute walk
ACCESS Tuesday, 10.00–20.00; Wednesday to Sunday, 10.00–17.00

Annette Gigon & Mike Guyer 1995

Greater Zürich

Annette Gigon & Mike Guyer 1995

Judd Fountains, Winterthur

Many contemporary Swiss architects feel an affinity for the work of American artist Donald Judd. He and other minimalists are cited as influences more often than are other architects. The link appears especially close among the exponents, commonly subsumed under the label of *Neue Einfachheit* (new simplicity), criticised for reducing their architecture to mere variations on the box. Many find a kindred spirit in Judd's philosophy of art and his degree of abstraction eliminating personal experience in favour of universal principles of space. Judd's art stems from his belief in archetypal forms that have the capacity to communicate inherent meanings with respect to the site and its beholder.

The reorganisation of the Steinberggasse in the centre of Winterthur is the artist's largest public commission, though Judd never saw his project completed due to his death in 1994. The space is divided by the placement of three fountains over the length of the long and narrow square, aligning them with the existing old fountain. Judd even adopted the site's oval shape as the basic form of his fountains. All the fountains share a congruent basic form, but the basin, water surface and movement interact in such a way that gives each an individual, yet overall coherent, character. One gurgles, another murmurs, the third invites one to rest, while it keeps on babbling and chuckling to itself.

ADDRESS Steinberggasse, 9400 Winterthur
CLIENT Verein Judd Project
COST SF750,000
TRAIN to Winterthur, then a 10-minute walk
ACCESS open, though the fountains are covered during the winter

Donald Judd 1996–97

Donald Judd 1996–97

Sammlung Oskar Reinhart 'Am Römerholz', Winterthur

Some of Switzerland's most famous private art collections are in Winterthur. One of the names to which the city is most indebted is Oskar Reinhart, who was born into a family that was, and still is, devoted to supporting the arts. Reinhart kept his collection at the Römerholz, his private residence. He commissioned the same architect who had already built the villa to design a large picture gallery for his favourite art pieces – a collection of Old Masters as well as French paintings of the nineteenth century. An even larger number of predominantly nineteenth-century Swiss and German paintings was donated to the city and exhibited in the centre of Winterthur. In 1970, five years after Reinhart's death, his home and art collection were turned into a public museum under the patronage of the Swiss Confederation.

Annette Gigon and Mike Guyer, who already built the extension to the Winterthur Kunstmuseum (page 4.2), won the competition for the renovation and extension of the Römerholz. Renovation was necessary to improve the museum's infrastructure, lighting and security measures. The main intervention lay in the construction of three new exhibition rooms, so connecting the villa with the picture gallery. The different character of the exhibited art works also determined the sizes and proportions of the rooms. Large, lantern-like roof lights penetrate the interior and electronically controlled lamellas filter and diffuse the natural light.

Instead of making formal references to the existing buildings, all gestures on the outside are reduced to a minimum. Solid concrete walls delineate the cubic arrangement, which is capped by the roof-light construction. More subtle references to the existing buildings are found in the structure of the prefabricated-concrete façade. The copper sheets covering the roof of the old exhibition annex inspired the architects to

Annette Gigon & Mike Guyer 1997–98

Annette Gigon & Mike Guyer 1997–98

experiment with the possibility of an oxidised concrete façade. By adding limestone and copper during the casting process, oxidation quickly changed the concrete's colour to green. Almost like an alchemist's experiment, the accelerated oxidation allows the new volume to catch up with the ageing process of older buildings.

ADDRESS Haldenstrasse 95, 8400 Winterthur
CLIENT Swiss Confederation
STRUCTURAL ENGINEERING Deuring & Oehminger, Winterthur
COST SF6.5 million
SIZE 2400 square metres; museum 1000 square metres
TRAIN to Winterthur, then a 20-minute walk
BUS 3 to Spital, 10 to Haldengut
ACCESS Tuesday to Sunday, 10.00–17.00

Annette Gigon & Mike Guyer 1997–98

Annette Gigon & Mike Guyer 1997–98

Forestry Station, Turbenthal/Rheinau

In 1991, the Canton of Zürich asked Sumi & Burkhalter to design a proto-type for four wooden forestry stations. They proposed an 'assembly box' of three components: an office, a garage and an open shed, which could be freely arranged. The Turbenthal station was the first to be realised in 1993; a second one, in Rheinau, followed a year later.

At Rheinau the components form a court, while at Turbenthal the forestry station lies parallel to the contours of the hill, reinforcing the edge of the glade. The interior is clad in plywood and is equipped with built-in wooden furniture.

On the south-facing façade, office, garage and shed are joined by continuous red cladding. On the entrance side, vertical boards and a natural finish for the garage are juxtaposed with red-painted horizontal boards for the office. The box beams spanning 5 metres are supported by steel beams that rest on 8-metre-high tree trunks: the borders between architecture and nature are intentionally subdued.

ADDRESSES Forstwerkhof Turbenthal, Ramsbergerstrasse, 8488 Turbenthal/Forstwerkhof Rheinau Im 'Geissert' am 'Weberweg', 8462 Rheinau
CLIENT Canton of Zürich
STRUCTURAL ENGINEER H Hofacker & M Krebs, Zürich
GETTING THERE Trubenthal: TRAIN from Zürich or Winterthur to Turbenthal, BUS to Hehlhof, walk uphill toward Ramsberg, 300 metres into the forest. Rheinau: TRAIN from Winterthur to Marthalen, BUS to centre of Marthalen, walk 4 kilometres to the old school building in Ellikon am Rhein, 800 metres into the forest in an easterly direction
ACCESS open; telephone 052 385 38 79 (Turbenthal); 052 319 25 71 (Rheinau)

Sumi & Burkhalter 1992–94

Forestry Station, Turbenthal/Rheinau

Sumi & Burkhalter 1992–94

Wooden bridge, Nesslau

The reappearance of wooden bridges is a recent phenomenon. Credit must be given to a few specialised engineers, mostly living and working in mountainous regions, in combination with the development of new wood constructional techniques. The think tanks behind these innovations and developments are not big corporations with costly research laboratories but small offices run by a handful of skilled people, of which Walter Bieler's firm is a good example.

The wooden bridge set in the idyllic river landscape of Nesslau spans 30 metres across the river Thur and replaces the old steel lattice bridge of 1899. Thanks to the low weight of the wood and its high static strength, the existing abutments can still be used without reinforcement, in spite of today's higher load requirements. Taking into account the community's wish for local resources to be used, the bridge was built with wood from the local forest and constructed by craftsman living in Nesslau. Optimising the use of the trunks forms the theme for both structure and design. The support structure is compressed into a compact lattice of beams, pillars, plates and planks. The individual components fade into the background in favour of the powerful bridge structure. It is the profile of the asymmetric cross-section and the cantilevered walkway that give the bridge its unique character.

LOCATION Nesslau
STRUCTURAL ENGINEERING Walter Bieler, Bonuadnz
COST SF520,000
TRAIN to Nesslau, the bridge is 1 kilometre south of the station
ACCESS open

Walter Bieler with Ruedi Zindel 1996

Wooden bridge, Nesslau

Greater Zürich

Walter Bieler with Ruedi Zindel 1996

EMPA, St Gallen

Now in his mid-70s and building probably more than anybody else in the country, Theo Hotz is one of those successful Swiss architects who never formally studied the subject. Starting his office when he was 21 years old, he can look back on countless realised administrative and industrial buildings, some built at a stunning scale. With unbroken loyalty to modernism and a continuous interest in construction and technology, Hotz's buildings are characterised by compositional assemblies of elements and volumes, together with a *Baumeister* pragmatism to complete them as quickly and economically as possible.

The EMPA (Federal Institute for Material Testing) is perhaps his most substantial recent building (see pages 3.6, 3.46, and 4.24). Hotz puts most emphasis on the articulation of the façade. Elements of glass and metal are assembled in an extraordinarily precise constructional framework, giving the concrete an inner structure and a surprising lightness.

In this industrial building architecture is understood as an interdisciplinary process of composing functional, constructional and aesthetic qualities. It is a convincing and truly Swiss contribution to the economic demands of the 1990s to use contemporary production and assembly techniques under the watchful eyes of an old *Baumeister*.

ADDRESS Lerchenfeldstrasse 5, 9014 St Gallen
CLIENT Swiss Confederation
STRUCTURAL ENGINEERING Fürer, Bergflöd, Köppel AG, St Gallen
COST SF90 million
BUS 7 to Moos from main train station
ACCESS none; visible from the street

Theo Hotz 1993–96

Seestrasse housing, Horn

What you see is what you get: a box with attitude. Beat Consoni designed a straightforward and simple volume, which is planned and built with immaculate precision. The design is based on layered concrete floors supported by the central service zone, which in addition to the pilotis along the perimeter allows for a flexible room division in the apartments. While the northern façade on the main street is clad in large prefabricated-concrete slabs, all the other sides are glazed from top to bottom. Large sliding windows allow an immediate experience of the Bodensee and its surroundings, though all apartments share a roof garden to compensate for the absence of balconies. The basement, with parking spaces and various subsidiary rooms, is half sunk in the ground. The most intriguing detail is the gap between the terrain and the ground floor's cantilevered concrete slab. Seemingly without support, the building creates the effect of a clean-cut cube hovering just above ground.

ADDRESS Seestrasse 44, 9326 Horn
CLIENT GEWICO, Gmbh
STRUCTURAL ENGINEERING Alban Längle, Stuchen
SIZE 592 square metres
TRAIN to Horn
BUS St Gallen to Horn
ACCESS none; visible from the street

Beat Consoni 1993–95

Greater Zürich

Beat Consoni 1993–95

Liner Museum, Appenzell

This building is dedicated to the works of the two local painters, father and son, both called Carl Liner. Ten exhibition rooms were designed for their art while leaving open the possibility for temporary exhibitions. The spaces are simple and serene rooms that do not compete with the exhibited art for the visitors' attention. The shed roofs give an even illumination, while the metal roof cladding optimises the diffusion and reflection of light. The museum's formal quality mediates between the additive alignment of traditional saddle roof houses of the region and the shed roofs of the more recent industrial architecture of the periphery. The differences in width and height of the exhibition rooms result in unusual sheds tilted at varying angles. The treatment of the building's skin is a focal point: thin, sand-blasted chromium-steel sheets wrap around the façade and roof alike. The chromium fish-scales can also be read as references to the traditional wood-shingle façades still encountered around Appenzell. The use of a single material for the exterior cladding of a building seems to be on many architects' minds at the moment.

ADDRESS Unterrainstrasse 5, 9050 Appenzell
CLIENT Stiftung Museum Carl Liner Vater und Sohn
STRUCTURAL ENGINEERING Aerni & Aerni, Zürich
COST SF7 million
SIZE 1350 square metres; museum 650 square metres
TRAIN to Appenzell, then a 2-minute walk
ACCESS Friday to Sunday (seasonal changes); telephone 071 788 1800

Annette Gigon & Mike Guyer 1997–98

Annette Gigon & Mike Guyer 1997–98

Bicycle stand, Dietikon

Bicycle stands are not the most prestigious architectural objects. Although the fairly straight-forward requirements tend to limit the level of complexity, this stand is different.

Translucent glass is draped over the prefabricated concrete structure, leaving all details of construction visible. The large planes appear thin and vulnerable, and require a degree of care. Interestingly enough and against all expectations of the city council, little graffiti or vandalism have damaged the stand ... so far.

The stand is part of a series of other traffic-related buildings installed in front of the train station. The same building-kit was used in various combinations in an attempt to create an underlying coherence. Ueli Zbinden sees his role as building on an urban tradition of post-war modernism. Zbinden is convinced that people have become used to their surroundings, despite the considerable drawbacks of the architectural heritage of the 1960s and 1970s. He believes that by integrating these elements into his work, he can generate a feeling of confidence into the built environment.

ADDRESS Bahnhofplatz, 8953 Dietikon
CLIENT City of Dietikon
STRUCTURAL ENGINEERING Sennhauser, Werner & Rauch AG
COST SF3.5 million
SIZE 730 square metres
TRAIN S-Bahn to Dietikon
ACCESS open

Ueli Zbinden 1990–92

Bicycle stand, Dietikon

Ueli Zbinden 1990–92

ABB office building, Baden

The ABB industrial site is the largest urban development in the city. Theo Hotz's comb-shaped office building has an eight-story-high backbone and four identical six-story 'teeth'.

ABB demanded an architecture to reflect the company's high-quality engineering achievements. Hotz was predestined for this role, profiting from his experience in hi-tech office buildings. His project won the competition due to its low cost per workspace (SF44,200), and for its airy spaces flooded with light and, at times, stunning interior vistas. The most distinct part of the building is the 33-metre-tall tower that houses the main entrance, elevators, a representational staircase and meeting rooms. Its cubic volume is fully sheathed in glass, making no distinction between façade and roof surface. It is 15 metres taller than any other building in the area and (too) obviously signifies modern corporate power. At night it glows like a lantern light bulb and is visible for miles.

Hotz has skilfully created an attractive new office building for 2100 workers while exercising his usual tight control on construction, cost and timing. The whole compound was built in two years.

ADDRESS ABB Areal Haselstrasse, 5401 Baden
CLIENT ABB Power Generation Ltd
STRUCTURAL ENGINEERING Minikus Witta & Voss, Baden
COST SF125 million
SIZE 49,500 square metres
BUS 1 from Bahnhofplatz
ACCESS none; visible from the street

Theo Hotz 1993–95

Theo Hotz 1993–95

Au Langmatt School, Brugg-Lauffohr

The confrontation with the vast rear façade of the school takes the viewer by surprise. The building's main attraction is the 10-metre high exposed concrete wall that stretches the full length of the 100-metre façade. A delicate geometric pattern traces the *in-situ* casting process and emphasises the sensuousness of the material. Compensating for the blocked view of the valley below, the rectangular surface resembles a constructivist painting – erratically dispersed perforations pattern the tableau while the cut-out openings, flush with the façade, enhance this effect.

The L-shaped concrete foundation is flipped up at 90 degrees and forms the building's backbone. Service and circulation zones are placed in the vertical section while workshops are in the horizontal part, forming the basement. The lower corridors are illuminated by light shafts – beautifully reflecting the light by the coloured glass fragments that cover the ground. Oriented towards the meadow and the river lies a fully glazed volume that contains the classrooms. Slender pilotis and a glass façade differentiate the front from the rear.

The architects have succeeded in contributing an innovative extension to a conglomerate of four existing school buildings. The office, which has been around for some 25 years, first attracted international attention for the school in Wohlen (1988) – a collaboration with the then relatively unknown Santiago Calatrava.

ADDRESS Langmattstrasse, 5200 Brugg-Lauffohr
CLIENT City of Brugg
STRUCTURAL ENGINEERING Dr U Gränacher, Brugg
SIZE 5200 square metres
BUS to Sommerhaldenstrasse
ACCESS school hours: 9.00–17.00

Burkard, Meyer & Partner 1994–95

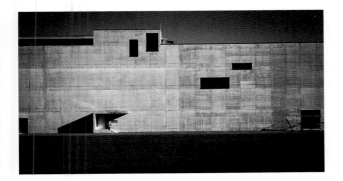

Burkard, Meyer & Partner 1994–95

St Anthony Roman Catholic Centre, Egg

Roughly a decade ago, Miroslav Šik won the competition for the extension of the St Anthony Roman Catholic Centre. Besides the new auditorium, much attention was devoted to the amendment of the prevailing liturgical condition as well the enhancement of its spatial experience.

MH/TH Our interest ... lies mainly in the underlying attitude that generates the buildings. More recently the architect is often seen as something like a pop star; you take a position believing that the signature of an architect does more harm than good ....

Miroslav Šik I read that often about myself. I think that traditional architecture has a signature as well, but it is not as obvious. I don't work without interpretation. But it is not easily visible when measured with the instruments of modernism. Someone who knows a little about the older architecture sees that I'm working with tradition – quite boldly really. But it is on a level that usually doesn't interest the modern architect. I certainly weaken contrasts, that is true. I take dominant parts, sometimes spatial configurations, sometimes materials, sometimes configurations of ridge and eaves or façade alignments. The more I take over the more I am forced to defamiliarise. The two buildings [see also page 9.24] that we are discussing here are both religious buildings, which means that the range of possible interventions gets even smaller. The respect when working on a religious building or site permeates every pore in my body and sits deep in my bones. What's important about the St Anthony centre is its historical value much more than its architectural value. It is the shingles, the specific roof shapes and colours of particular materials which are its most obvious characteristics. I feel that I had no choice but to take these over. Then I work with the modular construction ... with the metaphor of the Ark. And

Miroslav Šik 1992–97

Miroslav Šik 1992–97

here is where a significant difference to the existing structure lies. I have altered and changed the ensemble but the new things are not especially emphasised, let's say they are pretty modest. It is like variations in classical music, you have a very clear given topic and I vary accordingly within.

The effort in the St Anthony Centre is very different to the one in Morges. There it was first necessary to create an order. Here, on the other hand, it was very much given. I highlighted some aspects, revitalised them. The further away from the actual church, the more I distance myself from the given order; the less obedient I am, the more leeway I allow myself.

MH/TH What does the term traditionalism mean to you? Can you identify with it?

MŠ Well, yes I do have to label myself somehow and inherent in this label are some things dear to me. I am not after preserving a particular world nor after the prevention of a certain course of events. I am much more thinking of the regional architecture in the post-war period. It is modest and holds back and still loves lots of things about the old world. I want to change things but not in a big and loud way. My architecture likes to import things, too, but quietly.

ADDRESS Pfarreizentrum St Antonius, Flurstrasse 10, 8132 Egg
CLIENT Roman Catholic Church
STRUCTURAL ENGINEERING Basler & Hofmann, Ing. & Planer, Zürich
COST SF8 million
TRAIN Forchbahn to Egg
ACCESS open; telephone 01 984 11 10 (Sekretariat Pfarrhaus)

Miroslav Šik 1992–97

Greater Zürich

Miroslav Šik 1992–97

Esslingen town centre

The small town of Esslingen is the terminus of the Forchbahn, connecting Santiago Calatrava's Stadelhofen Station in Zürich (page 3.20) with the commuter towns on the outskirts. The competition, in 1989, asked for a dense development including train station, post office, restaurant, shopping facilities, offices and housing, at a time when architectural focus on inner cities shifted to a concern with the neglected periphery.

According to the architects, the periphery is neither a landscape in a true rural sense nor is it inscribed with architecture in a traditional urban manner. The project is an architectonic response to its surroundings, based on a reading of topography, nature, orientation and view. The underlying belief is that a coexistence of natural environment and dense urban conditions can be attained. The rivulet separates public from private and forms the boundary for 50 planned housing units. South of the rivulet, generous open spaces mark the public ground where the train station, bus stop and post office are located.

ADDRESS 8133 Esslingen
CLIENTS Canton of Zürich; Community of Egg; Forchbahn AG; Rehalp Verwaltungs AG; Basler & Hofmann Ing. & Planer AG
STRUCTURAL ENGINEERING Basler & Hofmann, Ing. & Planer AG, Zürich
TRAIN Forchbahn to Esslingen
ACCESS open

Angélil/Graham/Pfenninger/Scholl Architecture 1990–96

Angélil/Graham/Pfenninger/Scholl Architecture 1990–96

Grison

School, Mastrils

Mastrils is a small agricultural village spread out along the foothills of the broad Linth valley. Having no real centre, it was clear that this new public building should be a unifying and mediating element between the different parts of the village. The programme called for a new primary school, kindergarten, multipurpose hall and municipal office. To absorb the differences in height, five successive layers are stacked on top of one another, firmly embedding the complex in the steep hillside and the village structure. The building's prominent position allows for entrances not only at the top and bottom, but also from the sides on each level. All this resulted in a formally simple but compact solution that creates a unity while still attending to various functional needs. The building's core is an open cascading corridor that connects the different levels and allows a true sense of the steepness of the site. Large windows at the end of each storey give views of the valley below. Long strip windows extending over the full length of the building accentuate the already pronounced horizontal alignment of the terraces, while the solid, washed concrete finish and the absence of a base firmly anchor the building to the mountainside.

ADDRESS Schul- und Gemeindezentrum Mastrils
CLIENT Community of Mastrils
STRUCTURAL ENGINEERING Branger & Conzett AG, Chur
COST SF8.7 million
SIZE 2782 square metres
TRAIN to Landquart then BUS to Mastrils or a 10-minute walk to Mastrils
ACCESS school hours: Monday to Friday, 9.00–17.00; by appointment at the town hall in the same building

Jüngling & Hagmann 1994–95

Grison

Jüngling & Hagmann 1994–95

Transformer station, Seewis

The transformer station has not been built to interact with the casual visitor and, as such, it has no inherent human scale. Like a massive rock – a remnant from the glaciers that created the landscape – it sits there withstanding the fierce elements while radiating an elemental power.

There is something 'cool' about this brutal, hermetically sealed mono-lith, which is placed on a left-over piece of grass between the roadways of a heavily travelled intersection. Nothing protrudes or interrupts its undemanding presence except narrow ventilation slits and the fine line marking massive concrete doors.

ADDRESS Kantonsstrasse-Prättigauerstrasse, 7212 Seewis
CLIENT AG Bündner Kraftwerke, Klosters
STRUCTURAL ENGINEERING Jürg Conzett, Chur
COST SF800,000
SIZE 415 square metres
TRAIN to Landquart, then to Seewis, then a 10-minute walk
ACCESS by appointment only

Conradin Clavuot 1993–94

Conradin Clavuot 1993–94

Sunniberg bridge

At the beginning of the twentieth century, the works of civil engineers in Switzerland emerged from obscurity due to the achievements of engineers such as Robert Maillart. His concrete bridges, in particular, have received international acclaim for their aesthetic and architectural qualities.

Christian Menn's first bridge was constructed in the post-war period when new methods in prestressed concrete allowed engineers to span hitherto inconceivable distances. Menn established himself as one of Switzerland's leading civil engineers, due to his technical skill and also on account of the conceptual and aesthetic qualities of his bridges.

Sunniberg bridge, Menn's most recent project in Switzerland, is the most prominent construction on the Klosters bypass. The thin lane is suspended by cables attached to four double pylons and stretches across the Serneus valley in a horizontal arc 62 metres above the ground. The concrete prongs appear separated and stabilised by the narrow road. The remarkable thinness of the pylons is made possible by the curve of the bridge, which relieves the horizontal cross forces.

Menn has had fruitful collaborations with architects on several occasions: in the case of Sunniberg bridge, with architect Andrea Deplazes.

ADDRESS on the Práthigauerstrasse 30 to Klosters and Davos
CLIENT Tiefbauamt des Kantons Graubünden
STRUCTURAL ENGINEERING concept Professor Dr Christian Menn
SITE SUPERVISORS Bänziger & Köppel and Brändli & Partner
COST SF17 million
ACCESS open

Christian Menn, Andrea Deplazes 1996–98

Christian Menn, Andrea Deplazes 1996–98

Kirchner Museum, Davos

German expressionist painter Ernst Ludwig Kirchner spent the last 20 years of his life in the health resort of Davos – he committed suicide in 1938. After capturing images of modern life in urban Berlin in the 1910s, the artist was inspired by Davos and its mountainous surroundings to depict the serenity of life in the Alps. The Kirchner Museum, which opened in 1992, not only houses a large collection of the painter's estate, but also exhibits other artists of his period.

The museum is a conglomeration of freely arranged cubes occupying a prominent position along the main street and opposite the classical Belvedere Hotel. It responds formally to the town's historical structure of predominantly flat-roofed buildings, many from the 1920s.

The building is divided into four higher exhibition rooms, which are connected through a lower circulation passage. This circulation zone, finished in fair-faced concrete and much lower in height, leads from the entrance to the exhibition spaces. The low ceiling and the difference in material make the step from the corridor to the white-plastered, light and high exhibition rooms full of contrast. The exhibition rooms are modelled on nineteenth-century picture galleries with their evenly distributed skylights. Lighting presented the architects, Annette Gigon and Mike Guyer, with considerable difficulties. At Davos, natural light at this altitude (1500 metres) would be either too glaring or too dark because of the surrounding mountains. By letting daylight enter sideways from clere-story windows, the architects also took into consideration the winter snowfalls, when a regular rooflight would be covered by snowdrifts for much of the time. Sensors regulate a natural and artificial lighting system that ensures even distribution of light in the exhibition rooms. This explains why the upper semi-transparent section is not an actual storey, as it might appear from the outside; a third of the whole height of the

Annette Gigon & Mike Guyer 1989–92

Grison

Annette Gigon & Mike Guyer 1989–92

cube houses the custom-made hi-tech lighting system.

The museum plays with glass in all its forms – transparent, matt, polished, broken – depending on its function. It is transparent in the large windows framing views of Davos, matt and profiled on the façade where it protects the layer of thermal insulation, and matt in the skylight diffusing the incoming light. A layer of broken glass fragments replaces the usual gravel on the roof and it sparkles and reflects the sunlight, so enhancing the crystalline character of the building.

The glass containers and their various uses of glass deceive the eye. They play with the viewer's expectations to open up spaces – so offering insights and outlooks. On the façade, however, where the only function of the glass is to protect the insulation panels, it neither reveals the views of the inside nor brings in any light. The large windows on both ends of the circulation corridor, on the other hand, frame 'real' images of the townscape, views that Kirchner frequently painted.

ADDRESS Promenadenstrasse/Ernst Ludwig Kirchner Platz, Davos (081 413 23 12/413 22 02)
CLIENT Kirchner Stiftung Davos (donation of R M Ketterer)
STRUCTURAL ENGINEERING DIAG-Davoser Ingenieure AG, Davos
COST SF11.5 million
SIZE 2200 square metres
TRAIN to Davos, then a few minutes walk
ACCESS Tuesday to Sunday, 14.00–18.00; 15 July and 30 September, 10.00–12.00, 14.00–18.00

Annette Gigon & Mike Guyer 1989–92

Grison

Annette Gigon & Mike Guyer 1989–92

Sports Centre, Davos

Ice hockey is one of Switzerland's most popular winter sports. Especially in Davos, a long tradition of first-ranking ice hockey teams can be traced, so when the old wooden skating-rink from the 1930s was destroyed by fire there was no question of not building a replacement.

Annette Gigon and Mike Guyer's competition-winning project underwent several fundamental changes up until its realisation in 1996 because of considerable programmatic reductions and changes in overall volume. The proposed building was lowered by one floor and a costly metal grill-work façade was rejected in favour of wooden cladding. The finished exterior cladding is now a kind of two-layered horizontal fence, consisting of an outer layer of unfinished weathered clapboard that contrasts starkly with an inner layer of brightly coloured, painted wood.

The two-storey sports centre is a simple, stretched, rectangular volume, bordering the ice rink on one side and the main parking area on the other. It contains a variety of facilities such as restaurants, changing rooms, club facilities, conference rooms, guest rooms, apartments and garages. The stadium seating is integrated into the façade and it reveals the building's concrete structure, which remains covered by the wooden cladding almost everywhere else.

Colour often plays an important role in the works of the architects, and they have collaborated with several artists on other projects. In the case of the sports centre, their third and most recent project in Davos (page 5.8), this interest in a strong colour concept appears in its most prominent form. In collaboration with artist Adrian Schiess, a colour concept for the exterior as well as the interior was developed. A bright orange, complementary blue and light yellow are used on the façades, while six other colours are used on the inside surfaces: dark blue, *framboise*, white, apricot, light green and turquoise. They refer to sports and

Annette Gigon & Mike Guyer 1992–96

Grison

Annette Gigon & Mike Guyer 1992–96

Sports Centre, Davos

athletes, both of which are associated with strong, bright colours. A system of random attribution determined which panels and surfaces on wall and ceiling should be painted in which colour. On the interior, the colours are ever-present and take on spatial qualities in the way light and reflection divide the spaces into coloured segments. This is most apparent on the second floor where associations with the work of the American artist Dan Flavin are evoked by the roof lights which bathe the long corridor with a sequence of luminescent, coloured segments. When night-time mutes the colour on the exterior, it is the illuminated rooms of the interior that radiate colour to the outside. Colour is thus used to emphasise and signify the activity and life of the sports complex both to the outside and the inside.

ADDRESS Talstrasse 41, 7270 Davos Platz
CLIENT Davos Tourismus (Kur- und Verkehrsverein)
STRUCTURAL ENGINEERING DIAG-Davoser Ingenieure AG, Davos (building); Branger & Conzett AG, Chur (grandstand)
COST SF19 million
SIZE 3955 square metres (Geschossfläche), 18,695 cubic metres
TRAIN to Davos, then a few minutes walk
ACCESS open

Annette Gigon & Mike Guyer 1992–96

Grison

Annette Gigon & Mike Guyer 1992–96

Home for the elderly, Masans

Ten years ago, Peter Zumthor's projects were known only by insiders. The international attention following his Sogn Benedetg Chapel (page 5.56) brought him instant fame, and along with Herzog & de Meuron and Diener & Diener he became an early exponent of the newly discovered Swiss-German architecture. No architectural tourist is likely to visit Switzerland without stopping in Grison to see some of Zumthor's buildings. Trained as a cabinet-maker, Zumthor studied interior design before enrolling in the architectural programme at the Pratt Institute, New York. His academic and practical background allows him to follow abstract ideas while retaining a strong literal sensibility. A strong feeling for site, material and history also lie at the core of his architecture, while the sensuousness of his materials and a perfected craftsmanship are his trademark.

Homes for the elderly can be quite dreary. This residential home in Masans near Chur, however, is an exception. The 21 small apartments are intended for those still in good health but who might need some help with daily chores. It is also next to an old people's nursing home whose facilities can be used when required.

Zumthor did not conceive the building as a symbol loaded with messages, but rather as an envelope and a background for the life that goes on in and around it. In this residence the main objective was to provide a home for the elderly in a relaxed, rural environment. Like a rock, the elongated rectangular volume lies at a right angle to the softly sloping terrain, allowing the inhabitants to view the Alps from their individual balconies. Though of great simplicity, there is nothing rigid or cold about the home. Larch wood, cream coloured tuff stone and concrete are all commonly used in the regional architecture and, therefore, are familiar to the inhabitants. Open and closed, light and heavy characterise the north-facing façade with the main entrance, which is structured by rhyth-

Peter Zumthor 1989–93

Grison

Peter Zumthor 1989–93

5.18

mically alternating large windows and tuff walls. At the heart of the residence are wide, open corridors on both storeys that not only provide access to the apartments, but also function as communal space. Independent of weather or season, the residents are free to sit and talk in the corridor, where they can at the same time overlook the coming and goings in the courtyard.

ADDRESS Cadonaustrasse 71–75, 7000 Chur
CLIENT Stiftung Evangelisches Alters- und Pflegeheim Masans
STRUCTURAL ENGINEERING Engineering Partnership Jürg Buchli, Haldenstein
BUS 4 from train station to Cadonaustrasse
ACCESS none; visible from the street

Peter Zumthor 1989–93

Grison

Peter Zumthor 1989–93

Grison

Cemetery, Fürstenwald

Cemeteries have traditionally been located immediately behind the church in the centre of towns and villages. The new cemetery of Chur, however, had to be outside the city because of spatial constraints.

MH/TH What did you base your design on?

Günther Vogt The further you move away from urban areas like Zürich and Basel, the more you start to get a feeling for the overpowering presence of nature. While cities desperately try to bring in nature, here people feel a need to distance themselves. A good example for this are the different materials used for tombstones: the natural stones commonly used in urban areas just wouldn't make sense up here. Instead, people use crosses made out of metal.

In Fürstenwald, our job was first to level the steep terrain and then to find the best spot for the chapel and the mortuary. It was important to underline the elevated position, removed from the city, while at the same time looking down upon it. Accentuating the drop on the one hand and the distance to the forest on the other gives the cemetery its own identity, being neither city nor nature. We believe that cemeteries are the strongest expression of culture. Fürstenwald is an important place which will have to find its own tradition, as every person from Chur will most likely come here sooner or later.

MH/TH How did you collaborate with the architect Zinsli? We find it difficult to say where your work stops and his begins. Is this characteristic for the blurring of boundaries between the two professions?

GV We actually like the fact that you can't keep the two apart any more. … In this case, we worked together on the project from the very beginning. But such a collaboration is a rather recent development. Ten years ago landscape architects were only called in at the very end to work

Kienast & Vogt with V Zinsli 1992–96

Grison

Kienast & Vogt with V Zinsli 1992–96

5.22

on the left-over spaces around or behind a house – to add a touch of green. There was a clear hierarchy in the process. Now the relationship has changed considerably, and we encounter a complete reversal. The profession of the architect is under enormous pressure these days. At the same time the work of landscape architects has gained significantly in importance and recognition. The question of context, of how a building relates to its surroundings, has become as important as the architecture itself. Today's social and ecological awareness is due mostly to the unrelenting discourse generated by the eco- and women's movements of the 1970s. They are, you see, the main promoters of our profession. There is also a wide-spread malaise due to a hi-tech burn out: glass and stainless steel alone do not make a city liveable. It's not surprising that the theme of plants in various forms has started to appear in the works of architects and visual artists.

ADDRESS Fürstenwaldstrasse, 7000 Chur
CLIENT City of Chur
COST SF6 million
BUS 2 from Chur train station to Fürstenwaldstrasse
ACCESS open

Grison

Kienast & Vogt with V Zinsli 1992–96

Grison

Kienast & Vogt with V Zinsli 1992–96

Enclosure for Roman ruins, Chur

The creative act in which a work of architecture comes into being goes beyond all historical and technical knowledge. Its focus is on the dialogue with the issues of our time. At the moment of its creation, architecture is bound to the present in a very special way. It reflects the spirit of its inventor and gives its own answers to the questions of our time through its functional form and appearance, its relationship with other works of architecture and with the place where it stands.

The answers to these questions which I can formulate as an architect are limited. Our times of change and transition do not permit big gestures. There are only a few remaining common values left upon which we can build and which we all share. I thus appeal for a kind of architecture of common sense based on the fundamentals that we still know, understand and feel.

Peter Zumthor, in 'A way of looking at things', *a+u*, 1998, p. 2

ADDRESS Seilerbahnweg – next to Brämbrüesch-Bahn, 7007 Chur
CLIENT Amt für Bundesbauten
STRUCTURAL ENGINEERING Jürg Buchli, Haldenstein
BUS to Markthalle in direction Felsenberg
ACCESS open Tuesday to Sunday, 10.00–12.00, 14.00–17.00. Key can be picked up at the Rhätischesn Museum, Hofstrasse 1, 7000 Chur; telephone 081 257 28 89

Peter Zumthor 1985–86

Grison

Peter Zumthor 1985–86

Technikum, Chur

Chur's industrial zone is only stumbled on when searching for a petrol station or fast-food restaurant when travelling to and from the motorway. It is an architectural no man's land – a wild array of buildings lines the through-roads.

Instead of resorting to the usual architecture used for such institutions, Jüngling & Hagmann reacted to the environment in a more direct manner. Their project reinterprets the surrounding industrial architecture.

The school resembles an armadillo and stoutly occupies its site on a corner, its weathered copper panels forming the scales of the metal skin. As the boundary demarcating public space remains undefined and the asphalt from the street extends all the way to the building's main façade, visitors leave the street and enter the building without any mediation. Although natural light falls into the open space from the roof lights, one still cannot escape the feeling of being locked in a vault. The central hall's solid walls offer no view of the outside and a massive coffered grid rhythmically structures the interior. The ground floor contains all public functions such as a library, cafeteria and administration centre, while the upper light-filled floors house the classrooms.

ADDRESS Ringstrasse/Pulvermühlestrasse, 7000 Chur
CLIENT Ingenieurschule HTL, Chur
STRUCTURAL ENGINEERING Branger & Conzett AG and Raetia AG, Chur
COST SF32.7 million
SIZE 8458 square metres
TRAIN to Chur then BUS 2 to Ingenieurschule
ACCESS Monday to Friday, 8.00–20.00 during term time

Jüngling & Hagmann 1992–93

Grison

Jüngling & Hagmann 1992–93

Train and bus station, Chur

Reminiscent of nineteenth-century railway station architecture, this fully glazed hall spans the tracks of Chur's central station and links the old town to the north with the newer quarters on the south side. It is the most prominent part of a large-scale urban development around the station and gives shelter to a newly constructed deck that accommodates the bus station. Visitors travelling to Grison by public transport most likely arrive under this huge glass construction before departing for their mountain resort.

When travelling up the escalators from the platform to the upper deck, the traveller enters the large, open, transparent hall set amid the spectacular alpine landscape. At night, this perception is reversed: when seen from above, the hall is transformed into a large, softly lit volume clearly marking the centre of the city.

ADDRESS Gürtelstrasse 14, 7000 Chur
CLIENT PTT
STRUCTURAL ENGINEERING Edy Toscano, Zürich; Ove Arup & Partners, London/Paris; P Rice and A Hughes, London
COST SF25 million
SIZE 5000 square metres
TRAIN to Chur station
ACCESS open

Brosi & Obrist 1991–92

Grison

Brosi & Obrist 1991–92

0-Energy House, Domat/Ems

Dietrich Schwarz practically took on the role of an engineer when designing the two houses with close to zero heating requirements. Highly developed solar technology determined all formal and technical aspects.

Transparent insulation, a domestic warm water system and photovoltaic installations are the main components of this heat- and electricity-producing machine. The extensive research into optimising energy fixed design parameters such as the arrangement of the façade, the depth of the buildings and practically all materials. On the south side the insulation transforms direct sunlight to heat, which is absorbed by the concrete wall. The heavy wall stores it and eventually passes it into the room. Where there is no sunlight, there is no need for an absorber. The north façade is composed of only transparent insulation, compensating for the lost light on the opposite side. Conventional projects tend to stick solar technology on to already designed buildings; Schwarz uses its requirements to determine form. This pioneering project deserves attention, but it also seems obvious that basing architectural decisions entirely on technical requirements risks buildings with limited spatial qualities.

ADDRESS Via Calundis 8, 7013 Domat/Ems
CLIENT Jürgen Schwarz, Domat/Ems
STRUCTURAL ENGINEERING Branger & Conzett AG, Chur
COST SF1.3 million
SIZE 198 square metres
TRAIN to Domat/Ems
CAR 7 kilometres from Chur
ACCESS none; visible from the street

Dietrich Schwarz, Dr Werner Platzer 1995–96

Grison

Dietrich Schwarz, Dr Werner Platzer 1995–96

Mortuary, Bonaduz

The choice of the peculiar site, inside the mound behind the church, was based on a discomfort about the siting of a house for the dead too openly by a kindergarten. It is a fascinating location with equally powerful associations: grave, tomb, underworld. And then, in the search for the appropriate mood, the architects do the unexpected: the mourner enters a tall portal, follows a dark tunnel and eventually finds nothing but light. 'It should evoke life, not death', they explain. 'Both opposites need to be present.' The two contrasting spaces collide: the rectangular, dark concrete tunnel, about 15 steps long, hits the white, tall, perfectly elliptical space at its centre. An opaque door marks the intersection. The central space rises out of the mound, flooded by light entering at an angle from the top, which in return emphasises the vertical dimension. Unfortunately the two-room cabinet for the laying out of the deceased is an intrusion into the elliptical space. However, the density of the vibrant brightness resists the obtrusion by this element, which creates a discord in the otherwise perfectly shaped room.

ADDRESS Via Sogn Gieri, 7402 Bonaduz
CLIENT Community of Bonaduz
STRUCTURAL ENGINEERING Toni Cavigelli AG, Domat/Ems
COST SF900,000
SIZE 112 square metres
TRAIN to Bonaduz
ACCESS open; key can be obtained from the town hall

Rudolf Fontana & Christian Kerez 1993

Mortuary, Bonaduz

Grison

Rudolf Fontana & Christian Kerez 1993

Chapel, Oberrealta

The brightness and simplicity of the single-cast concrete building stand in stark contrast with the lush green foliage of the surroundings. Isolated on a ridge, the chapel overlooks the river Hinterrhein.

The straightforwardness of the chapel is striking – a prototypical, single-room house with unadorned concrete walls on a rectangular plan, the roof pitched at 45 degrees and no ledge. A small cross above the entrance marks the building's religious purpose. One enters the shell through a cut-out opening over a detached step; a minimal vertical slot in the south façade allows in a trickle of light. Beneath the shell are the remains of the original eighteenth-century chapel dedicated to St Nepomuk, patron saint of rivers. The unpredictability of the Hinterrhein caused the locals much trouble. At the turn of the century, however, the river bed was corrected and the saint's protection became redundant and the chapel fell into ruin. It might well be that the villagers' guilt was the initial motivation for the commission of the new building on the old site.

Rudolf Fontana and Christian Kerez's challenge lay in the redefinition of the site and much of the power of the project lies in its ambiguity: part chapel, part shelter for the remains of the original chapel, it also functions as a signifier marking a site that preserved its significance over time.

ADDRESS Oberrealta, 7408 Cazis
CLIENT Kapellenverein Realta
STRUCTURAL ENGINEERING Toni Cavigelli AG, Domat/Ems
COST SF50,000
SIZE 13 square metres
TRAIN to Rothenbrunnen
CAR to Oberrealta
ACCESS open

Rudolf Fontana & Christian Kerez 1994

Rudolf Fontana & Christian Kerez 1994

School, Paspels

This uneasy monolith, with all its angles and elements a little out of balance, appears as if a landslide had upset its neat arrangement. However, its strength lies in this disrupted rigidity. The arrangement of the plan is fairly simple: three classrooms and a smaller subsidiary room are placed in different corners around the central space. The discongruent arrangement and irregular geometry of the rooms give each level a completely different appearance, which leaves the visitor bewildered, trying to understand the underlying logic. These manipulations cleverly create spaces of appealing perplexity that eventually diffuse the building's centre. Without falling into the trap of making stylistic references, the school reflects various aspects of a local building tradition still very much alive today in this fairly remote and tiny village. A massive single-layer concrete shell encloses the additive system of rooms. The classrooms, clad in larch wood, have the atmosphere of cosy living rooms and stand in stark contrast with the bare and echoing central circulation space, which was left in concrete.

MH/TH This project seems to abandon the issue of the box by subversively dismantling and distorting it from within.

Martin Steinmann [architectural critic] I am surprised to hear you say this. Isn't this project confirming the box issue? This is only one way to deal with this topic. … Olgiatti carries the tension from the outside to the inside.

MH/TH … which is a typically Swiss phenomenon. Things happen on the inside …

MS The way you say it sounds negative. I find this an extremely exciting aspect.

MH/TH No, it is not meant entirely negatively. It is meant with regard to

Valerio Olgiati 1997–98

Valerio Olgiati 1997–98

other cultures like, let's say, Holland, where things are often turned outwards. In Switzerland, we've always had this Calvinistic stance of being outwardly modest. ... The Swiss baroque had white façades and most beautiful tiled stoves on the inside.

MS You mean to keep one's composure. But remember, an explosion that does not go off on the outside has an impact which is ten times as strong on the inside. I personally do not think much of extroverted architecture that tries to create a forced happiness. Those who cannot appreciate such boxes have an insufficient cultural understanding. I think the whole 'box' issue is only at the beginning. There is much more potential that needs to be exploited, especially in this inner strength.

ADDRESS Oberstufenschulhaus Paspels, 7417 Paspels
CLIENT Politische Gemeinde Paspels
STRUCTURAL ENGINEERING G Descaper, Ing. HTL, Paspels
COST SF3.8 million
SIZE 9917 square metres
TRAIN to Reichenau/Tamins
BUS to Reichenau/Tamins-Paspels
ACCESS Monday to Friday, 8.00–12.00, 13.30–16.00; closed Wednesday afternoon

Valerio Olgiati 1997–98

Grison

Valerio Olgiati 1997–98

Traversina footbridge

Although it is possible to catch glimpses of the wooden footbridge from the opposite side of the valley, actually to get there one needs to follow a steep and winding path. The footbridge is part of the Veia Traversina, a path that follows the traces of a Roman trail and part of an 'eco-museum' that stretches along Viamala gorge.

Over time, rock and mud slides destroyed all traces of the old footpath at the bottom of the narrow Traversina ravine. Since it would have been difficult as well as costly to reconstruct the crossing in the wet and eroded terrain, a new bridge was proposed to link both sides of the ravine. The bridge spans 47 meters atop surviving Roman stonework at two points which satisfied the geological requirements for the abutments.

The footbridge has to overcome obstacles usual for such alpine structures, namely a remote site with difficult access, restrictive economic constraints and a short construction time. In many respects, design and construction were taken to the limit by the unconventional methods used. The weight of the bridge's substructure was limited to the load-carrying capacity of the most powerful helicopter available; and in the design process subjective judgements were necessary. As such, the bridge has a very light space-frame with panelled side rails acting as stiffening girders. Predominantly larch wood and non-corrosive steel cables were used. To minimise further the construction weight of the assembly units, the structure is divided into a light substructure and a much heavier superstructure, designed both to stiffen and protect the substructure. Since the substructure rests only on two supports, it needs to be stabilised against torsion by the superstructure, which consists of two-ply panel-stiffening girders as side rails and a horizontal glulam beam under the walkway. Wind resistance was also a crucial factor in determining the shape of the bridge. During a strong gale the lower chord on the upwind side could

Branger, Conzett & Partner AG 1996

Traversina footbridge

Grison

Branger, Conzett & Partner AG 1996

lose its tension and the walkway could slightly rotate around the down-wind lower chord.

All wood was left untreated and since weather-exposed timber is of limited durability it was necessary to design the bridge in such a way not only to protect the most important structural elements, but also to allow the replacement of the exposed parts.

The substructure was erected at an assembly yard 500 metres from its final destination. Mounted on scaffolding towers, the structure was assembled piece by piece, requiring a high degree of accuracy since the length tolerances of the steel diagonals were only 5 millimetres. The weight was always carefully monitored and all parts were protected from the rain, which would have increased their weight substantially. When finished, the substructure was lifted by helicopter and moved into place in 30 minutes. Parts of the superstructure were then fixed *in-situ*. During the course of writing this book, the bridge was destroyed by an avalanche in 1999, and plans for its reconstruction were still under discussion.

ADDRESS Schweizerische Landeskoordination 754250/171000
CLIENT Verein KulturRaum Viamala, Chur
STRUCTURAL ENGINEERING Branger, Conzett & Partner AG
COST SF310,370
SIZE length 47 metres, width 1.2 metres, height 38 metres
TRAIN to Thusis ROAD to Thusis or Viamala
ACCESS Veia Traversina is a signed footpath from Thusis railway station to Sils i.D. and through the Viamala Gorge to Viamala bus station. The hike takes 2–3 hours and walking boots are recommended. Alternatively, skip along the road to Thusis. For information on reconstruction, contact Verein Kulturraum Viamala; telephone 081 252 81 23.

Branger, Conzett & Partner AG 1996

Grison

Branger, Conzett & Partner AG 1996

Museum, Flims

The white cube is a striking landmark amid the hotch-potch of chalets; naked, but for a sheer layer of white paint, it stands stoutly in the centre of this mountain resort. What at first sight looks like a very modern building dates from the 1870s and stands as a legacy of the late local architect Rudolf Olgiati, eminent proponent of Grison architecture.

After decade-long discussions about the derelict house, Rudolf Olgiati's will decided the building's fate. He offered to dedicate his entire private local-history archives to the community, on condition that the building be renovated according to his specifications: it had to be white, and it had to be publicly accessible. His son, Valerio, entrusted with the project, took a radical approach; by removing roof, portico, window frames, all interior structures and creating 33 almost identical punctured openings, the building was endowed with a strong sculptural quality.

Once inside visitors find themselves surrounded by a new, entirely wooden interior. Olgiati resumes work on the 'house within the house' theme of his earlier school in Paspels (page 5.36) by playing on the contrast between rough stone shell and serene interior.

ADDRESS 7017 Flims-Dorf
CLIENT Community of Flims
STRUCTURAL ENGINEER Conzett Bronzini Gartmann AG, 7000 Chur
COST SF960,000
SIZE 1690 square metres
BUS from Chur to Flims Dorf
WEBSITE www.dasgelbehaus.ch
ACCESS during exhibitions, seasonal opening hours; telephone 081 936 74 14

Valerio Olgiati 1998–99

Valerio Olgiati 1998–99

School, Vella

So far, this is the most important project by Bearth & Deplazes, whose architecture is characterised by a formal simplicity and an innovative use of standard materials. Even though the building's exemplary energy-saving qualities were not the basis of the design, the architects have proved that ecologically sound construction has less to do with costly, hi-tech systems than with an ingenious use of given functions and materials.

MH/TH Energy-saving concepts seem to be *en vogue*. Does it go without saying that today these aspects are incorporated into the design?

Andrea Deplazes Not at all. There is a growing awareness, but more on a technical than on an architectural level. The ecological aspect is important, but I would never use it as the sole basis for a design. It's more important for us to find the inherent idea of a site to generate the design process. Generally, financial parameters leave architects little leeway, they force them to become inventive, to keep on exploring … it's under these circumstances that you might discover that a wall is more than just a wall ….

MH/TH Vella, in that case, could be better described as a lo-tech rather than a hi-tech building …

AD … actually there's no tech at all! Only what is needed anyway; it's just a normal building! The 20-centimetre concrete of the outer walls derives from structural requirements and is all that is needed for optimal energy storing. We got really interested in the energy-saving aspect once we realised that we already had all the necessary preconditions and needed only to apply them correctly.

MH/TH … and there's no heating in the building, right?

AD No heating whatsoever. The only installation is the single ventilation source that circulates warm air throughout the building. Large

School, Vella

Grison

Bearth & Deplazes 1994–98

windows bring in light and produce heat, which is stored by the sheer mass of the building. ... The floors are solid stone slabs from stock leftover from Vals. The enlarged surface of the ribbed ceiling, which was cast *in-situ*, stores energy more efficiently, while improving acoustics. In the end, calculations showed our version to be even cheaper than a conventional ceiling serving the same functions. The challenge lies in finding the right balance.

MH/TH Your work is often described as part of a new Grison regionalism?

AD It's too easy to sum up all Grison architecture under one label. I dislike this labelling and stereotyping. We all draw from our personal experiences. Today traditional Grison architecture is often misinterpreted as being homey and atmospheric. ... We are not re-animating a forgotten architectural tradition, that would be totally wrong, ... society has changed so much. Grison is not a place where time has stood still, even though that's the promoted tourist image. It's not just a beautiful holiday resort with only friendly people. We are in fact interested to deconstruct this stereotypical idyllic image. What we're interested in is independent of its location, be it a city or rural village.

ADDRESS 7144 Vella
CLIENT Gemeinde Vella, Oberstufenschulverband Lugnez
STRUCTURAL ENGINEERING Casanova & Blumenthal, Ilanz
COST SF9.2 million
SIZE 16,000 cubic metres/2500 square metres
TRAIN to Ilanz, then BUS to Vella
ACCESS school hours: Monday to Friday, 9.00–17.00

Bearth & Deplazes 1994–98

Bearth & Deplazes 1994–98

School, Duvin

There are not many villages as remote and untouched by industrialisation and tourism as Duvin. Positioned on steep terrain far above the valley terminating in Vals, the tiny village has the most spectacular panoramic view that, in itself, is worth a trip. Gion A Caminada, a farmer's son and native to the similarly situated village of Vrin, has received considerable attention in recent years for the development of a traditional, solid timber construction unconcerned with the all too common nostalgic preservation usual with its use. Thanks to modern techniques, the architect has greatly expanded the potential of hybrid construction techniques. In Vrin, he has built a series of structures, such as a recent multipurpose hall or a building kit for stables and barns, all aimed at the sustainable development of village structures.

The school in Duvin is captivating for its simple realism. It offers neither a breathtaking spatial experience nor an aesthetic elegance or immaculately done details. Its appearance is generated not only by local resources – namely timber and local craftsmanship – but also by a logic based on functionality. Built as a three-storey complex, the building naturally finds its place in the picturesque village centre.

ADDRESS 7112 Duvin
CLIENT Community of Duvin
STRUCTURAL ENGINEERING Branger, Conzett & Partner AG, Chur
SIZE 512 square metres
TRAIN to Ilanz, then BUS to Reichen and Duvin
ACCESS school hours: Monday to Friday, 9.00–17.00

Gion A Caminada 1994–95

Gion A Caminada 1994–95

Therme Vals

Until recently, people only knew Vals from the mineral water that carries the same name. Few had actually made their way to this remote, little village situated at the end of the valley. All of a sudden it has become the talk of the day, and international journalists and tourists are venturing there *en masse*. The hot spring has existed for a century, but only in the 1960s did the idea arise of building a hotel complex to attract more tourists. It never became as famous as other spa resorts and in the 1980s, when entertainment pools with wildly curving water slides and fake palm trees were *en vogue*, Vals' Hotel Therme was deserted and close to bankruptcy. The local municipality, which then became owner of the hotel complex, decided to take a bold step and build a new bath. The result is a bath of another, much subtler kind; it has no jets or slides but, instead, a primal exposure to stone and water.

The always immaculate details of construction are characteristic of Peter Zumthor's ambitious architecture. This requires rigorous control over the building process in combination with highly skilled labour. Prominent workers, such as Grison's state masonry champion, were hired to complete the difficult and meticulous construction – a composite of *in-situ* concrete and load-bearing granite from local quarries. What appears a massive, monolithic stone wall in fact consists of thinly layered slabs of local granite. Some surfaces are highly polished while others are left roughly hewn, bringing out the hidden sparkle of the green, shimmering stone in different degrees.

Viewed from the outside, the sharp-edged rectangular solitaire lies deep in the mountainside. The subterranean maze of solid rock, steam and cavernous baths is reachable only by a long access tunnel from the hotel. Stepping out into the bathing area, visitors enter a world of stone and water, of darkness and light. Continuous cave-like corridors meander

Peter Zumthor 1990–96

Grison

Peter Zumthor 1990–96

Therme Vals

through a structure of large stone blocks – which have entrances cut into them and that lead to individually carved-out spaces. Streaks of sunlight drift along the walls from linear gaps in the roof and 16 small, blue roof lights above the main indoor pool diffuse a bright blue light.

Zumthor often talks about the sensuousness and sensuality of architecture, and if any recent building can be described in such terms, it is this one. The mahogany-clad changing rooms have more in common with a boudoir than the average dressing room in a sports centre, and the sauna and steam rooms are virtual dark rooms with contours of people hidden behind wafts of steam and the different zones closed off by heavy, black leather curtains. The petal pool gives the feeling of swimming in some mystical aphrodisiac, and while the sulphur-smelling water is ingested from the metal cups chained to a steel railing, the fire-red reflections on the wall of the narrow fountain room give, perhaps, a first glimpse of hell.

Vals really is different, it is a phenomenon ... in many ways. The visitor-count in the first year was more than double the most optimistic of estimates. Their ever-increasing number is a catalyst in the transformation of the entire economic structure of the village.

ADDRESS 7132 Vals
CLIENT Gemeinde Vals
STRUCTURAL ENGINEERING Engineering Partnership Jürg Buchli; Casanova & Blumenthal, Ilanz
TRAIN from Chur to Ilanz, then BUS to Vals
EMAIL therme-vals@bluewin.ch
ACCESS Monday, 7.00–21.00; Tuesday to Sunday, 7.00–20.00, until 23.00 for hotel guests only; closed end of April to beginning of June, and end of October to mid-December; telephone 081 926 80 80

Peter Zumthor 1990–96

Peter Zumthor 1990–96

Sogn Benedetg Chapel, Sumvitg

To me, the presence of certain buildings has something secret about it. They seem simply to be there. We do not pay any special attention to them. And yet it is virtually impossible to imagine the place where they stand without them. These buildings appear to be anchored firmly in the ground. They create an impression of being a self-evident part of their surroundings, and they seem to be saying: 'I am as you see me, and I belong here'.

Peter Zumthor, in 'A way of looking at things', *a+u*, 1998, p. 2

ADDRESS Chapel, 7175 Sumvitg
CLIENT Stiftung Sogn Benedetg
STRUCTURAL ENGINEERING Engineering
Partnership Jürg Buchli, Haldenstein
TRAIN from Chur to Sumvitg, then TAXI
or a 25-minute walk
ACCESS open

Peter Zumthor 1985–88

Sogn Benedetg Chapel, Sumvitg

Grison

Peter Zumthor 1985–88

School, Tschlin

The little, dark red school building at Tschlin is suspended in the air – it is almost as if the slightest tremor could send it sliding down the steep slope. The school's colour and prominent position in the densely structured village draw immediate attention to it. To work in such a small community demanded a clear awareness of the need of different groups using the hall: the school, village officials, sports clubs and local orchestra, which stressed the need for good acoustics. The result satisfied even international music connoisseurs. Investigations into the optimisation of natural light sources led the architects to place high window strips along the sides and four large windows offering views of the valley.

The colourful hall's façade is neither of wood nor plaster, but in fact is of painted cast-concrete. The school looks a bit odd as it sits there looking out over the valley, but at the same time its simple, rectangular volume and the shallow saddleback roof set it comfortably into its rural setting. What lies at the core of the architectural vision is the unpretentious use of every day forms and materials rather than highly construed *objets d'art*. This straightforward approach, which concentrates on a few essential aspects, creates sensitive translations of the commonplace.

ADDRESS 7559 Tschlin
CLIENT Gemeinde Tschlin
STRUCTURAL ENGINEERING Mayer, Sent
COST SF3.6 million
SIZE 4400 cubic metres/800 square metres
TRAIN via Saunedan to Schol-Tarasp, then BUS via
Strada to Tschlin
ACCESS school hours: Monday to Friday, 9.00–17.00

Bearth & Deplazes 1991–93

Bearth & Deplazes 1991–93

Ticino

La Congiunta, Giornico

'La Congiunta' – the marriage – is the example of a special relationship between art and architecture. The unusual union between the sculptures of Hans Josephson and the architecture of Peter Märkli has put the tiny village of Giornico on the map. Giornico, which lies at the bottom of the Leventina, has not been affected by tourism like so many other villages in Ticino. The landscape and the precipitous mountainsides do not allow much sunlight into the narrow valley bottom and most tourists heading south zoom past on the elevated motorway or railway.

La Congiunta is not really a museum in the conventional sense and those who expected red carpets and upholstered chairs will most likely be disappointed by the cold, fair-faced concrete walls. No one welcomes the visitor at the entrance – the key has to be picked up at the bar in the village restaurant. It is the product of an encounter between the distinct styles of architect and artist.

The stepped concrete volumes fit effortlessly into the rugged landscape, but the windowless rectangular blocks are not exactly inviting at first. Visitors have to go around the building before they can enter it through an austere steel door with a suspended step. Diffused natural light enters through a roof-light, casting a play of light and shadows on the walls. The interior arrangement of blocks reveals three independent main spaces and four smaller subsidiary galleries, each corresponding to specific phases in the sculptor's oeuvre.

There are no installations in the building: no heating, no artificial lighting, no floor coverings – only the crude materials, the bare essence of architecture. Märkli's language confronts visitors and engages them in a dialogue with the most elemental forms of expression in art and architecture. The architecture accompanies the sculpture's plastic expression with variations in spatial proportions, light and materiality, creating

Peter Märkli with Stefan Bellwalder 1992

Peter Märkli with Stefan Bellwalder 1992

distinct atmospheres and moods. Neither architecture nor art try to dominate the other, thereby creating a resonating, almost sacred feeling that is hard to grasp.

Another concrete structure, the Viadotto della Biaschina (Biaschina viaduct), lies only a few kilometres north of Giornico. It offers one of the most spectacular views of a 100-metre-high viaduct from below – and is definitely worth the trip.

ADDRESS La Congiunta, 6745 Giornico
CLIENT Stiftung 'La Congiunta'
COST SF800,000
SIZE 340 square metres
TRAIN from Bellinzona to Giornico. Ask in the Osteria-bar Giornico in the town centre for the key and directions. Then a 10-minute walk along the old Roman road
ACCESS open

Peter Märkli with Stefan Bellwalder 1992

Ticino

Peter Märkli with Stefan Bellwalder 1992

Municipal infrastructures, Iragna

In 1990 Iragna held a competition for a new town hall, a multipurpose gymnasium, the refurbishment of the existing school and an overall urban strategy. Raffaele Cavadini won with a precise urban analysis whose concept tried to unravel and strengthen the town's underlying structure. Almost a decade later the architect has realised three main interventions: the town hall, the mortuary and a public square. Cavadini has succeeded in fusing modernist ideas with the traditions of regional building: white concrete blends with local granite, and horizontal window strips are positioned amid heavy masonry. The project's concept is based on three squares, marking both ends and the centre of Iragna, positioned along the main road and the historical axis. A key role is performed by the town hall, an elongated building in front of the church.

Iragna was recently praised by critics as one of the most important contributions to Ticinese architecture of the 1990s. Cavadini's concept is a significant effort in sustaining and strengthening old village structures. The inventive strategy and precise interventions attempt to escape the fate of other towns where the struggle with migration results in either desertion of the populace or the surrender of the town's heart to tourism.

ADDRESS Iragna
CLIENT Municipality of Iragna
STRUCTURAL ENGINEERING P Regolati, G Masotti and W Perlini
COST SF1.6 million
SIZE 555 square metres
BUS from Biasca train station to Iragna
CAR motorway exit Biasca
ACCESS town hall, working hours only; mortuary, ask for the keys at the town hall office

Raffaele Cavadini 1993–95

Raffaele Cavadini 1993–95

Castelgrande, Bellinzona

Castelgrande towers over Bellinzona. Strategically positioned and standing in isolation in the middle of the Ticino valley, the massive rock bears witness to the interest of people from all ages. Romans, Northern Italian dukes and the King of France as well as leaders of the Swiss Confederation have left their mark: a palace, a church, towers, arsenals, a prison, annex buildings and a widespread system of battlements. Many restoration proposals were made after the hill was declared the property of the canton in 1925. It was only in the early 1980s, however, when a private sponsor unexpectedly offered SF5 million for the restoration of Castelgrande (the money was bound to a given time limit) that city and canton immediately started work on a programme.

Local architect Aurelio Galfetti took on the challenge of revitalising the fortress, which had become disconnected from the life of the city below, while retaining an imposing presence in the landscape. He also succeeded in his careful negotiations with the official body opposing his innovative concept. The Committee for Historic Preservation tended to favour a conservative reconstruction over a radical transformation. Galfetti, however, kept asserting his principle of 'preservation through transformation'.

The architect's transformation of the castle did not consider the buildings so much as the exterior spaces that turned the fortress into a park. He used the already existing materials of the site – rock, walls, lawn, battlements – to transform elements of defence into elements of peaceful relaxation. Galfetti did not see the park as an alignment of trees and bushes, but stressed its integration on an urban scale. A primary intervention was actually one of subtraction. Stripping the rock wall facing north on to Piazza del Sole of all vegetation gave it a bold architectural quality. The vineyards on the south-facing side, however, function as the

Aurelio Galfetti 1981–91

Aurelio Galfetti 1981–91

Ticino

Castelgrande, Bellinzona

continuation of the city rising towards the castle. The fortress buildings were restored and are now used as a reception hall, restaurant and exhibition spaces. The old walls were restored to their former volumetric strength and only a few new concrete sections were added, mainly in the restaurant, conference hall and a number of walkways.

Castelgrande consists of not only the buildings and spaces on the hill, but also the structured network of routes leading there. Besides the battlements and the steep footpath there is also the spectacular elevator from Piazza del Sole: a long, straight path enters the rock in a dripping crevice at the bottom of the mountain and ends in a cavernous space, which was widened and redesigned in concrete.

The renovation of Castelgrande is an intervention demonstrating that even historical monuments must be updated if they are to survive.

ADDRESS Piazza del Sole, 6500 Bellinzona
CLIENT Republica Cantone Ticino
STRUCTURAL ENGINEERING E Vanetta, Lugano
COST SF20.5 million
SIZE 35,000 cubic metres
TRAIN to Bellinzona, then a 2-minute walk
ACCESS Castelgrande: daily, 10.00–24.00; museum: daily, 10.00–18.00

Aurelio Galfetti 1981–91

Castelgrande, Bellinzona

Aurelio Galfetti 1981–91

Ticino

Swisscom, Bellinzona

Situated on the outskirts of Bellinzona, Ticino's capital, is Mario Botta's new administrative centre for Swisscom.

MH/TH You have described peripheries as difficult situations.

Mario Botta Yes, that's true but in Bellinzona the periphery is consolidating itself. In a certain sense I wanted to create a point of reference for the neighbourhood. New streets are planned and I had the idea of giving a centre or a focus to the periphery, which hasn't got a form. I wanted to give it a structure – an element which gives strength.

MH/TH In your church projects we can see a symbolic dimension in the use of the circle, but how should one understand it in other projects, such as banks, apartment blocks or the Swisscom?

MB Circle, square ... you can do all kinds of things with these elements. It's wrong to say all rectangular buildings are the same, the same applies for the circle. One has to be careful – Mogno [page 6.26], for example, is an absolute circle: an extraordinary element was needed to confront the mountain. In Tamaro [page 6.30] it's not a circle – it is the head of a nail entering the mountain – another signification again. ... I'm just interpreting a situation.

MH/TH And in this project? Does the circle have the function of a piazza?

MB No, no here it's quite different again. Here is a huge building which despite many surrounding buildings takes up the idea of a block perimeter development with an interior court. It emphasises the street grid, but at the same time there is a visual link to the Castelgrande [page 6.8], which I consider to have priority. Breaking open the block was important to establish a connection with the old part of the city. I chose the circle, however, because I wanted to avoid dark corners in the court, so the round element allowed me bring in more light.

Mario Botta 1992–98

Swisscom, Bellinzona

Ticino

Mario Botta 1992–98

Swisscom, Bellinzona

MH/TH Everyone talks of the changing role of the architect. As teacher and co-founder of the new architectural school in Mendrisio, what is your vision for the future?

MB The whole profession has drastically changed – for everyone. I only do 50 per cent of what I used to do for a project. I cannot maintain an all-encompassing supervision of the sites any more. We concentrate on the project's conception and leave the execution to others.

The Accademia is born out of the conviction that there needs to be a completely different approach to answer the complexities of modernity. Every problem demands a dozen experts and consulting engineers. ... To be able to react to this complexity and today's fast pace there needs to be greater stress on humanistic disciplines, not technical studies. The Accademia teaches philosophy, aesthetics, contemporary art history, anthropological history, history of the terrain, architectural history. ... Only if you are familiar with these problems will you be able to tackle the solutions in practical life. The Accademia is born out the need to fill this cultural void, a cultural void which exists in Switzerland and also in Italy.

ADDRESS Via dei Gaggini, 6500 Bellinzona
CLIENT Swisscom Immobilien AG
STRUCTURAL ENGINEERING Ing. Balmelli & Filippini and Ing. Messi & Serafino, Bellinzona
COST SF82 million
SIZE 27,800 square metres
ACCESS office hours: 8.00–12.00, 14.00–17.00

Mario Botta 1992–98

Mario Botta 1992–98

Ticino

Palazzo Franscini, Bellinzona

Luca Ortelli's project, the result of a competition held in 1988, has caused quite a stir. Although heavily criticised for being conservative, we appreciated the complex for its poised calm and well-proportioned spaces. It marks a strong contrast with Mario Botta's massive Swisscom building just a few hundred metres away (page 6.12).

Palazzo Franscini houses the historical archive and cantonal library. The complex is composed of several blocks arranged around open spaces and a park. The volume containing the archives and library, characterised by its large, central atrium, forms the core of the complex. It is reached by a pedestrian alley and an open court flanked by two parallel blocks containing the offices of various institutions.

MH/TH Your work doesn't fit the label of what is generally considered typical Ticino architecture. Where do you see the differences?

Luca Ortelli It was not as if I set out to do something radically different when I first started working on the project. But if your aim is to do a quiet architecture, which can integrate itself within the context, you are somehow radically opposed to Ticino architecture, which is characterised (if I'm not wrong) by a much stronger presence in its relationship with the surroundings. Naturally this kind of architecture played a very important role 20 years ago, but I'm much more interested in subtler and quieter ways of approaching a context. I'm very fond of Scandinavian architecture. Much of what can be considered Romance or Mediterranean architecture, I rediscovered by studying the work of [Gunnar Erik] Asplund and other Swedish architects.

MH/TH In your project we find an assemblage of architectural fragments, which refer to recognisable urban locations: there is an alley, a court, a square … and always the feeling of already having been there.

Luca Ortelli 1993–98

Palazzo Franscini, Bellinzona

Ticino

Luca Ortelli 1993–98

Palazzo Franscini, Bellinzona

LO ... you're right, this is another important point in our work: to make buildings which are not strange to a context, an architect must build recognisable spaces. That's why in the end the building is a collage of different, but very clearly identifiable, spaces. ... An aphorism by [Auguste] Perret illustrates very well what we consider to be of crucial importance for building today: 'Celui qui, sans trahir les matériaux ni les programmes modernes, aurait produit une oeuvre qui semblerait avoir toujours existé, qui, en un mot, serait banale, je dis que celui-la pourrait se tenir pour satisfait'.

MH/TH What about your use of colour?

LO To avoid building a large monolith we decided to articulate the volumetric composition in different smaller volumes and to use colour to give the complex a recognisable unity. We wanted a quiet colour and chose a light yellow, reminiscent of the sand along the nearby river. Of course, the surprise comes upon entering the most important space, the atrium, and it was here that we decided to apply strong colours. The idea was to combine local architectural elements together with unexpected, rich colours.

ADDRESS Amministrazione Cantonale Dipartimento dell'Istruzione e della Cultura Archivio Cantonale, Viale Franscini 30a, 6500 Bellinzona
CLIENT Republica Cantone Ticino
STRUCTURAL ENGINEER Studio Ceresa Rezzonico Gervasoni, Bellinzona
COST SF30 million
BUS from train station to 'Arti e Mestieri', then a 300-metre walk
ACCESS Monday to Friday, 8.00–11.45, 13.30–17.00

Luca Ortelli 1993–98

Palazzo Franscini, Bellinzona

Ticino

Luca Ortelli 1993–98

Monte Carasso

Despite international fame, Luigi Snozzi has hardly been given the opportunity to realise his numerous competition-winning designs. What stands out in his œuvre are the experiments in urban planning he has pursued over the past 20 years in Monte Carasso.

His 1979 proposal for the renovation and conversion of a sixteenth-century monastery into a primary school and other communal facilities marked the beginning of Snozzi's close involvement with the restructuring of Monte Carasso. For him it was crucial to give the town a new centre to create a sense of local identity. A masterplan for the town and several other buildings followed: the gymnasium (1984); Raiffeisen Bank (1984); the conversion of the convent (1987–93); the large housing block facing the motorway (1996); houses and the redevelopment of the cemetery.

His architecture and research on the city is concerned with establishing parameters of construction valid for the entire context. Monte Carasso's building regulations – reduced from approximately 120 to five – are revolutionary compared with those in effect elsewhere in Switzerland:

Rule 1 Each intervention has to be designed in accordance with existing architectonic and urban structure. A committee evaluates the typological and morphological structures and the quality of the proposition.
Rule 2 Densification is achieved by abolishing all minimal distance regulations as well as by raising the number of storeys allowed.
Rule 3 Clear definition of the public space: boundary walls are mandatory with a maximum height of 2.5 metres.
Rule 4 Each new project calls for verification of the regulations. If a good project cannot be realised because of a regulation, the regulation is subject to change.
Rule 5 Maximal reduction of all regulations.

Luigi Snozzi 1979–96

Ticino

Luigi Snozzi 1979–96

These rules are obviously risky from a legal point of view, as so much depends on the individuals and subjective judgements. The public support and pride behind this project can only be explained by Snozzi's admirable powers of persuasion. 'Aesthetic control' over the form and materials has been eliminated in favour of rules restricting only the elements that define both private and public spaces. Judged more important than the individual plots are the resultant open spaces. Emptiness, the unbuilt space, constructs the greatest urban reality in a system determined by constantly changing factors.

In Snozzi's urban projects the individual architectural object steps back in favour of a unified structure. Falling into neither conservation nor rejection of the existing structures, Snozzi shows that it is possible to build in historical contexts without giving up precise architectural principles. Recent years have also seen the realisation of projects by other renowned Ticinesi architects such as Mario Botta and Roberto Briccola.

Interestingly, certain material and constructive principles, such as exposed concrete structures or flat roofs (not usually popular with the public), have almost become the rule. This exceptional acceptance, or even appreciation, of classic modern architecture has surprised many, and it is especially notable because of the total liberty given to architects in their use of the architectural language.

ADDRESS 6513 Monte Carasso
TRAIN to Bellinzona then BUS
ACCESS open

Luigi Snozzi 1979–96

Luigi Snozzi 1979–96

Multipurpose building, Losone

The Tendenza, believed by many to have reached a dead-end, is again attracting international attention not least due to Livio Vacchini's latest buildings: his own house in Costa (1993), the controversial post office in Locarno (1996) and, most importantly, his gymnasium in Losone.

The ambiguous character of this monolith fits right into the present architectural discussion. The building, playing on the absence of scale, goes to the very limits of its material and construction. Point of view, light and weather conditions provoke metamorphoses in the apparent weight and solidity of both columns and volume itself: it can be read as either a closed mass or a filigree box made out of fragile shafts. The walls consist of identical columns, which stand as far apart from each other as is possible without the use of a lintel. The columns on the outside of the glass, seem to support nothing, and a sense of gravity is effaced. The poetic charge of this building lies in the elemental essence of its simple form.

A sacred atmosphere permeates the interior of the gymnasium – an immaculate glass hall filled with light. The building evokes martial allusions, but avoids falling into monumentalism. Vacchini manipulates symmetry, rhythm and proportions and, though applying similar elements as in the post office, achieves a much more convincing architecture.

ADDRESS Via Arbigo, 6616 Losone
CLIENT Federal Military Department, Bern
STRUCTURAL ENGINEER Andreotti & Partners, Locarno
COST SF9.8 million
SIZE 3500 square metres
ACCESS none; restricted military area

Livio Vacchini, Mauro Ventti, Marco Azzola 1995–97

Multipurpose building, Losone

Ticino

Livio Vacchini, Mauro Ventti, Marco Azzola 1995–97

Church, Mogno

On 25 April 1986 an avalanche destroyed the seventeenth-century church of St John the Baptist in Mogno. Situated in a tiny village at the end of Val Maggia, the controversial new church is emblematic of Mario Botta's endeavours. With this project, his first church, the architect returned to the essentials of his tireless exploration of the relationship between the geometry of architecture and topography, between solid walls and precise openings, between physicality and light.

Mario Botta This project was initiated by a group who said that the church had to be reconstructed. Their motivation was very beautiful. At first I wondered why they wanted a church in a place where no one lives any more. They said they didn't want to give the future generation a place which is poorer than the one they knew. It's a very extraordinary justification; I was speechless. Then I said all right, I'll build you a new church which will last a thousand years. So I chose to build it in stone. There was never an open discussion as to what the church should look like, and when I showed the project to the public, there were people who asked me to reconstruct the old chapel. I said this was wrong; why should I try to redo a church from the seventeenth century with the technology of the twentieth? ... thus the polemics started only after and not before the project commenced. Now we are constructing the square in front of the church. It is a jewel ... a square with a 30-centi-metre thick white marble floor – its like walking on the Parthenon.

MH/TH A trivial question perhaps, but thinking of your architecture, asso-ciations with stripes cannot be avoided – where does this come from?

MB I've also built many buildings without stripes! But let me tell you where they come from. ... You see, stripes are the riches of the poor in rural cultures. You have red and white stripes on the buildings to

Mario Botta 1992–96

Mario Botta 1992–96

separate the houses from the stables. The house was often adorned with colour, painted windows and stripes in red from the blood of slaughtered pigs. You can find that in all Mediterranean architecture, in Siena, etc. I, however, use them because I believe that buildings should always have two dimensions: one of the landscape and the other more urban or domestic scale. My projects are often of monumental size, so I feel the need to give them a human dimension, to give evidence of the work of mankind. I like the idea that a building is made up of one structural layer on top of the other and there's nothing better to underline this but stripes.

MH/TH Can architecture also be political?

MB Let me answer you with a quote from Walter Benjamin: 'The political value of a literary work is its literary value'. So, the political value of an architectural work is its architectural value. If you do something which addresses thousands of people, it is political. If you do something that fails to communicate, it isn't of any political value. I don't believe that there is a direct political value in architecture.

ADDRESS 6696 Mogno, Frazione di Fusio, Vallemaggia
CLIENT Mogno Church Reconstruction Association
TECHNICAL ARCHITECT Giovani Luigi Dazio
STRUCTURAL ENGINEERING Ing. Lombardi, Locarno
SIZE 178 square metres
BUS from Locarno to Fusio
ACCESS open

Mario Botta 1992–96

Ticino

Mario Botta 1992–96

Chapel, Monte Tamaro

In 1990, the owner of the Monte Tamaro cable-car company asked Mario Botta to build a chapel in memory of his late wife. He envisioned a building that would enhance the setting while, simultaneously, activating the mountain top.

The new chapel – a fruitful collaboration between Botta and the painter Enzo Cucchi – sits on the ridge of the mountain overlooking the surrounding valleys at an elevation of 1500 metres. The chapel's access routes dramatically culminate in the belvedere, revealing a panoramic view. As if extending into space, the bridge eventually achieves solidity in the cylindrical volume at the end. The result is a hybrid construction metaphorically blending a tower, a bridge and a church.

MH/TH You wrote that the most difficult task with this project was to find the site?

Mario Botta Yes, when I went up there with Mr Cattaneo, there was just the little restaurant. I started to look for a site further up because I was interested in hollowing out the mountain and designing only one façade. I asked him where I should put it and he answered that I could put it wherever I wanted to! You see, that was really difficult. Usually we are only given little plots of land and then have to interpret. Where do you start when you have a whole mountain to choose from? I mean, I could virtually build wherever I pleased because there were no limits imposed by land ownership. Then I discovered a ledge marking the end of the footpath running down the mountain towards the existing restaurant. That's when I started designing the chapel as an imaginary extension and termination of this road. Visitors and hikers would have a pathway, which the mountain itself could not provide, as well as a marvellous new vantage point offering views of the valley below.

Mario Botta 1992–96

Ticino

Mario Botta 1992–96

MH/TH You have built all kinds of buildings and are considered a successful architect ….

MB Wait, wait … can I tell you one thing? They tell me that I've built a lot – that's fine. But if I make a list of all I've really built, including the good and the bad, I get a list of 40 buildings. The other day I met a local architect of whom no one talks and … he's built 200 houses in the Ticino! I have made about 300 projects, but actually only built 40! It might seem like I build a lot, but compared with the norm I actually build very little. It is very curious … I suppose my buildings make a lot of noise and then people think I build a lot!

MH/TH What kind of project do you dream about building in the future?

MB I'd love to build a convent! A convent with the theme of silence and contemplation. I'm intrigued by the idea of the complete isolation of a whole institution. Absolute seclusion. Twenty-four hours a day, all year round. Only the architecture and the people – both charged with spirituality … that I would love to do … rather than office buildings. … But you know the life of an architect is mysterious … if you want something you don't get it and when you least expect it, something appears out of nowhere!

ADDRESS Alpe Foppa, Monte Tamaro, 6802 Rivera; tel.: 091 946 22 53
CLIENT Egidio Cattaneo
STRUCTURAL ENGINEERING Ing. Passera & Pedretti
SIZE 184 square metres
TRAIN to Rivera, then a 5-minute walk to the CABLE-CAR for Monte Tamaro, daily 8.30–17.00
ACCESS December to March, June to October; telephone 092 946 2303

Mario Botta 1992–96

Chapel, Monte Tamaro

Ticino

Mario Botta 1992–96

Monte Lema Radar Station

Perched on top of Monte Lema against the backdrop of undulating mountain tops, the radar station pays reverence to the wide-open sky. Avoiding a gesture of conquest, Pietro Boschetti did not deprive the mountain of its natural peak but, instead, situated his intervention a few metres below. The balloon hiding the radar installation softens the hostile nature of the structure, while adding a sculptural quality.

Having got this far, you could take the opportunity to hike on the ridge to Monte Tamaro (page 6.30); wear good hiking boots and have plenty of energy for the spectacular 5-hour walk along the Swiss–Italian border.

ADDRESS Stazione Migliéglia, 6986 Migliéglia
CLIENT Amt für Bundesbauten, Swiss Meteorological Institute, Swisscontrol AG
STRUCTURAL ENGINEERING Giorgio Ferrario, Ing. STS, Lugano
COST SF5.05 million
SIZE 210 square metres
BUS from Lugano or CAR to Migliéglia, then FUNICULAR to Monte Lema, daily 8.30–18.00 (17.00 from end of October–mid-November). BUS departs to Rivera at 17.00 and returns from Rivera at 17.40 daily until November
ACCESS terrace only; telephone 091 609 1168

Pietro Boschetti 1990–93

Pietro Boschetti 1990–93

UBS Suglio, Manno

Manno, Lugano's industrial suburb, has not much to offer besides its motorway exit and anonymous architectural landscapes. Nevertheless, an ever increasing number of commuters from Bellinzona, Locarno, Lugano and Chiasso find their way to this modern-day wasteland. For the architects, however, it seemed natural to set a strong urban nucleus in the prevailing sprawl.

Suglio is almost a small town in itself: this project, one of the largest ever realised in Ticino, provides work for 700 people and is in fact bigger than many surrounding villages.

It has two faces. From afar UBS's most recent administration centre appears like a castello: solid walls, a yellow fortification with corner watchtowers and windows like embrasures. The inner court of the U-shaped complex, however, is very different. The outer, solid brick wall is fragmented and dissolves into a filigree system of shiny metal blinds and glass. 'We are building today what will be the future tomorrow' was the bank's motto for Manno. The resulting architecture by Schnebli, Amman & Ruchat-Roncati is, however, committed to a classical and rational modernism in the tradition of Le Corbusier and Aldo Rossi. Functional and sincere, the interior design aims at a high-quality working environment and a flexibility in utilisation, and it never seems pretentious. While the architectural language is still indebted to classical modernism, on a technical level the future has really begun in Manno. As an energy-saving house the project is of pilot character and has won several awards for its environmentally sound construction. Optimal use is made of daylight and natural ventilation, while the large window surfaces and solar panels mounted on the roof capture solar energy. The rain water, stored in the pools in the inner court, is used for the toilets and cleaning, saving 50 per cent of fresh-water consumption.

Schnebli, Ammann & Ruchat, Menz 1991–97

Ticino

Schnebli, Ammann & Ruchat, Menz 1991–97

UBS Suglio, Manno

In the case of Suglio, cooling, not heating, was the main concern, as it usually gets very hot in Ticino during the summer months. Falling back on traditional room heights of 2.9 metres – 0.5 metres higher than normal ceiling heights nowadays – had a noticeable effect. The heat-buffer was above the heads of the people in an office, creating agreeable working conditions. It is quite an achievement that Suglio can do without air-conditioning. In the summer, ventilation flaps are opened at night and they are arranged in such a way that a draught passes through the offices. While at night the cool air reduces room temperatures, the bare concrete ceiling acting as a cold storage during the day, cooling the rooms during working hours when the ventilation flaps are closed. This, combined with sun shades and high ceilings, makes air-conditioning redundant.

Suglio's architecture shows how ecological architecture not only depends on the discovery of expensive and complex hi-tech systems, but also actually has very much to do with the rediscovery and reinterpretation of traditional building techniques.

ADDRESS Via Cantonale, 6928 Manno
CLIENT UBS, Zürich
STRUCTURAL ENGINEERING Arge, Luigi Brenni *et al.*
COST SF250 million
SIZE 49,000 square metres
CAR N2 to Lugano Nord
ACCESS open

Schnebli, Ammann & Ruchat, Menz 1991–97

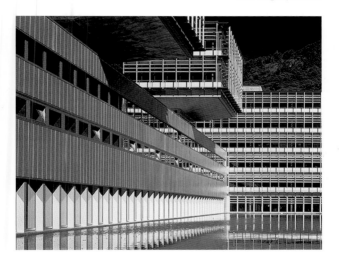

Ticino

Schnebli, Ammann & Ruchat, Menz 1991–97

Via Beltramina housing, Lugano

The Lugano-based architects are usually associated with stately mansions, not with social housing. Monochromatic white villas such as Casa Felder (1978), Casa Boni (1981) or Casa Kress (1986) are the basis of Mario Campi and Franco Pessina's fame. The 1990s have seen their engagement in several large-scale urban projects in Ticino and Zürich.

Campi & Pessina's winning design for a competition held by the municipality of Lugano in 1987 makes a strong statement about the amorphous identity of this part of town. The dominant seven-storey complex responds to the increasingly disintegrating neighbourhood with a rigorous formal reduction and structural clarity. The large U-shaped volume embraces an open courtyard, demarcating one of the few clearly defined public spaces in the area. A generous three-storey porticus facing the inner court alludes to traditional nineteenth-century northern Italian typologies. All ground floor space is given to commercial and public use: a coffee shop, exhibition spaces, offices and the headquarters of the Lugano police. The upper storeys contain 116 subsidised apartments.

ADDRESS Via Beltramina 3–9
CLIENT Cassi Pensioni della Citta di Lugano
STRUCTURAL ENGINEER Passera & Pedretti, Lugano
COST SF39 million
SIZE 21,000 square metres
BUS 3 from the centre of Lugano towards Parpassona
ACCESS none; visible from the street

Campi & Pessina 1992–95

Campi & Pessina 1992–95

Central Switzerland

Train station, Lucerne

After the old Lucerne train station was destroyed by fire, local architects Ammann & Baumann won the competition for platform extensions, a post office, shopping facilities, offices, housing and a school.

The site of the terminus is spectacular, but the restricted space between the platforms and the station square is dominated by bus shelters and leaves little room for a mediating space between the lake and the tracks. This lack of space forced most facilities to the subterranean concourse level. Pedestrians are pressed to follow this concourse if they want to avoid the heavy traffic on the street level.

Santiago Calatrava's style is most obvious in the extraordinary glazed portico, even though he had also designed the canopy over the loading area in the post office at an earlier stage of the project. The powerful main façade is characterised by the spindle-like steel props and the expressive precast concrete elements, giving the entrance hall an organic feeling reminiscent of his Stadelhofen station in Zürich (page 3.20). Supported by the steel spindles are the concrete elements, connected by a continuous beam and almost canopy-like cornice. Steel beams and mesh support the glass roof, suspended from the front portico and not, as might be expected, from the station front.

Calatrava's role in the overall project is small in comparison, but it is the engineer's aesthetic that makes this terminus memorable.

ADDRESS Hauptbahnhof, Lucerne
CLIENT SBB
STRUCTURAL ENGINEERING Dr Santiago Calatrava
TRAIN to Hauptbahnhof, Lucerne
ACCESS open

Santiago Calatrava/Ammann & Baumann 1983–89

Santiago Calatrava/Ammann & Baumann 1983–89

Culture and Congress Centre, Lucerne

On 12 June 1994, a national vote turned down a proposed new amendment to the Swiss constitution to support the arts. The people of Lucerne voted on the same day, but decided in favour of the project for a new Culture and Congress Centre and granted the biggest building loan ever in Lucerne – SF94 million. That it was possible to unite a whole city behind such a non-conventional and daring project in a time of economic uncertainties was only attainable due to a rigorous public relations campaign. The Swiss Design Award 1997 was given to the city's former mayor Franz Kurzmeyer and sociologist Thomas Held. Kurzmeyer's visionary cultural politics and Held's clever concept of integrating all parties involved into all relevant decisions at all stages, promoted the widespread trust of being part of something big and important. It was largely due to these two men's personal engagement that the city's population could be rallied to vote in favour of the centre. The new landmark took on forms under the watchful eyes of the whole city and the weekly guided tours of the construction site soon had to be increased.

Jean Nouvel's monumental centre is on the site of a former shipyard on the lake and in close proximity to the train station. The programme called for three facilities: a symphonic auditorium, two smaller halls and the Museum of Fine Arts. The building's relationship to the water, the city and music is the main theme of the design. The lake enters (at least pretends to enter) the building, letting the water's reflection and rebounding light play on the glazed façades and the enormous cantilevered roof. Views from foyers and footbridges all compose a series of carefully selected framings of the old town and the scenery of lake and mountains. The large symphony hall, designed in close collaboration with American expert Russell Johnson, forms the core of the complex and is a masterpiece in acoustics. The acoustics are particularly important

A J N, Architectures Jean Nouvel 1995–99

A J N, Architectures Jean Nouvel 1995–99

because of the prestigious International Music Festival hosted each year by the city. The acoustic installations are a visible and integral part of the architectural design: sound-diffusing plaster tiles are bonded to the impressive reverbrance chamber doors and balconies, while a mobile canopy functions as a sound-reflecting ceiling. The bold colour concept was hotly debated between the architect and the star-conductor Claudio Abbado, who refused to inaugurate the new hall during the festival if it were painted blue as planned. A compromise was found: all the walls were painted white and the possibility of flooding the room with coloured lights remains.

The three main wings of the centre differ in their purpose, structure and specific appearance, but they are joined under a single roof – the building's most prominent feature. The striking effect of Nouvel's intervention in this otherwise very traditional town is strengthened by the building's sheer size, its smooth glass façades and the enormous roof, which set it apart from the small-scale old town. The symphony hall was officially inaugurated in 1998, and the whole complex was handed over to the public at the turn of the century.

ADDRESS Europaplatz 1, 6005 Lucerne
CLIENT Trägerstiftung Kultur- und Kongresszentrum, Lucerne
ACOUSTIC ARCHITECT Russell Johnson, New York
STRUCTURAL ENGINEERING ARGE Totalunternehmer, Elektrowatt
Engineering AG; Göhner Merkur AG
COST SF200 million
TRAIN to Lucerne, then a 3-minute walk
ACCESS restaurant open; for culture centre and museum, see
www.kkl-luzern.ch

A J N, Architectures Jean Nouvel 1995–99

A J N, Architectures Jean Nouvel 1995–99

Herti School, Unteriberg

The project is the result of an open competition held in 1996. The existing school was to be extended with several classrooms, an assembly hall and a gym. The extension is designed as an autonomous building. The elongated structure is organised in three sections with flat saddle roofs of different heights. It is at the edge of the village against the backdrop of the impressive mountain scenery. Looking from the meadow to the north – thereby presenting only its short façades – the school matches the scale of the neighbourhood, forming a well-balanced ensemble with the church and the cemetery.

The wood shingle panelling of the façade is an old technique typically found in the Alps that has regained a new popularity in recent architecture in Switzerland. Together with the copper roof and anodised aluminium windows, its textile character gives the building a homogenous simplicity. The exposed concrete walls, slate tiles and larch woodwork of the interior create a natural and generous atmosphere.

ADDRESS Hertistudenstrasse, 8842 Unteriberg
CLIENT Bezirk Schwyz
COLLABORATOR Matei Manaila
COST SF10 million
SIZE 19,000 square metres
TRAIN to Einsiedeln, then BUS to Unteriberg
ACCESS school hours: 9.00–17.00

Stählin Helle Kämpfer 1999–2000

Stählin Helle Kämpfer 1999–2000

Sarna Kunststoff Holding, Sarnen

It is not a new phenomenon for architecture to be used to establish a corporate identity. A building, although it has no resemblance to the product, becomes the trademark itself. Currently, it is *en vogue* to mark such buildings with the signature of architectural superstars like Mario Botta, Richard Meier or Frank O Gehry. Accumulated, as in Vitra (page 2.2), they become something like a collection of masterpieces.

The new office building of Sarna Kunststoff Holding AG creates its identity with architectural means in a typically Swiss manner. The culturally rooted embarrassment of riches is manifested by giving nothing away before you enter the building. An almost overwhelmingly colourful central space is flanked by galleries connecting the offices. Here, the company represents itself as a corporation encouraging communication among the employees and creating a place they can identify with: coffee breaks and all circulation routes are around the intimate hall, which is the heart of the design. Typically for architects of Andreas Roost's generation, references to Le Corbusier are quite obvious. Ramps generate a *promenade architecturale* which gradually unravels the space. The application of primary colours dominates and creates an aura that changes under different lighting conditions and at different times of the day.

ADDRESS Industriestrasse, 6060 Sarnen
CLIENT Sarna Verwaltungs AG
STRUCTURAL ENGINEERING Plüss & Meyer AG, Lucerne
COST SF14 million
SIZE 5945 square metres
TRAIN to Sarnen
ACCESS by appointment only

Andreas Roost with P Ernst, S Schneider 1993

Central Switzerland

Andreas Roost with P Ernst, S Schneider 1993

Housing Aesch, Walchwil

Walchwil is a small community spread over a steep, south-facing slope overlooking the mountains and the lake of Zug. Inscribed into the site's topography lies Philipp Brühwiler's stepped-terraced housing, located at the upper edge of the village near the forest. The cascading layers, structured around a central staircase and divided into private, semiprivate and public areas, follow a grid-like symmetrical pattern. Generous individual terraces provide sufficient privacy, while semiprivate zones adjacent to the stairways promote neighbourly interaction. The curtain-like system of sliding larch wood shutters is the most expressive element. The light-permeable panels can be moved along the length of the glazed façade: they function as sun shades and as protection from the weather. The simple composition creates a visually arresting form derived from the topography of the site.

It might be of interest to compare this project with the office's earlier, fairly similar complex, built on the opposite side of Walchwil on Neuhausstrasse 1–5, Hörnulirain.

ADDRESS Chellenstrasse 14/16, 6318 Walchwil
CLIENT Baukonsortium 'Aesch'
STRUCTURAL ENGINEERING André Rotzetter & Partner, Zug
COST SF8.5 million
SIZE 1655 square metres
TRAIN to Walchwil
BUS 2 to Walchwil
ACCESS none; visible from the street

Philipp Brühwiler 1996–98

Philipp Brühwiler 1996–98

'Ort der Besinnung', Erstfeld

Just in time for the 150th anniversary of the Swiss constitution, the Canton of Uri resurrected the long-forgotten plans for a 'highway church'. An open competition was held for a 'place for meditation and contemplation' to people of all denominations and beliefs on the last service station north of the Alps. This place was to be a contemporary interpretation of the familiar roadside chapels. Inherent in the programme is an unsettling contrast between the purely functional service station and an apparently functionless place of meditation.

The winning project by two recent ETH-graduates is a minimal intervention. Reduced to the basic geometric forms of square and rectangle, a prominent 10-metre-high cubic volume faces the road, while a protected courtyard opens onto the rugged landscape.

What makes this project particularly remarkable is the design of the windows: thick double-glassed 'containers' are filled with fragments of broken green glass. This interpretation of traditional stained-glass windows has a beautiful effect: during the day sunlight filters through the glass casting atmospheric shadows in the interior. At night, on the other hand, the chapel is lit from the interior and appears from the roadside like a big lantern emanating a sparkling verdant light.

ADDRESS Gotthard Süd service station on N2, Erstfeld
CLIENT Stiftung 'Ort der Besinnung'
COST SF930,000
SIZE 100 square metres
ACCESS open

Guignard & Saner Architekten 1998

Central Switzerland

Guignard & Saner Architekten 1998

Hotel Furkablick renovation, Furka

At an elevation of 2431 metres, on top of one of the highest mountain passes in Switzerland, stands the Hotel Furkablick, which has withstood nature's fierce forces for more than 200 years. Owing to the harsh winter weather, the Furkapass is inaccessible for much of the year, but during the warmer summer months it is a popular point of repose for tourists, hikers, cyclists and Sunday drivers making their way up the winding road. Few wanderers stay for more than several hours, for the days when mountain hotels provided vital shelter on the long journey across the Alps are gone. As the car became the favoured means of transport, many of these stations lost their importance and sank into oblivion. The Hotel Furkablick was no exception: in the 1970s its doors were closed and it lay abandoned for many years. In the long run, however, this has been a stroke of luck. The hotel managed to escape the abominable fate of many others who underwent hideous renovations and it lay untouched until it was purchased and renovated by art gallery owner and publisher Marc Hostettler. Each year, he invites several artists to live and work in the hotel. Traces of 'Furkart' – the works of artists Beuys, Bill and Signer, among others – can still be found in and around the hotel.

In renovating his hotel, Hostettler left as much as possible in its original state and undertook only the most necessary interventions, which were done predominantly by himself. Today, one can still marvel at the cosy bedrooms where there are washstands with ceramic washbasins and pitchers of cold water, candle light and puffy down covers. Most striking of all is the old dining hall that now is a library on contemporary art. With ample space to lounge on the sofas next to the wood-fed tiled stove, it is easy to fall into a nostalgic mood. Not much seems to have changed since Goethe or Queen Victoria spent a few nights on the Furka as they crossed the Alps.

OMA 1991

OMA 1991

Though the name of Rem Koolhaas is enough to lure the cultural tourist all the way up to this remote place, it is not the architecture that strikes the visitor. OMA's structural intervention is small and unobtrusive, drawing little attention to itself.

In his best-selling book S, M, L, XL, Koolhaas mentions this project under 's' but it would probably be more appropriately placed in the 'XS' category. The most prominent feature of the project is the restaurant's metal entrance. Resembling the lens of an old box camera, the quadratic window looking out on to the Furka symbolises the hair-cross on a view finder. Koolhaas has taken the 'Furkablick' (view of the Furka) literally and makes it the focal point of his design. The pictorial views framed by the windows when one is inside are juxtaposed with full exposure to Furka's spectacular nature when sitting on the terrace.

ADDRESS Furkapasshöhe, 6491 Realp
CLIENT Marc Hostettler
POSTAL BUS twice daily from Andermatt and Oberwald; telephone 041 887 1188
ACCESS summer months only; telephone 041 887 0717

OMA 1991

OMA 1991

Bern and region

Kornhaus, Bern

Prominently situated in the old town of Bern, the venerable Kornhaus (a former grain storehouse of the eighteenth century) has recently undergone radical changes. Interventions by three different architects have been assembled under this roof. sam architekten refurbished the upper three floors, containing parts of the regional library, a small theatre and a grand public hall, which is used by the Forum für Medium und Gestaltung and the Architekturforum Bern. The ground floor Kornhaus Cafe was redesigned by Italian architect Christian Silvestrin in 1999, creating an elegant designer café under the arcades – a favourite hang-out for the trendy. The latest venture has been the renovation of the Kornhauskeller, originally a wine cellar, now transformed into a restaurant and a bar. Grego & Smolenicky's minimal interventions have retained and enhanced the unique character of the space. Identity markers, such as the large wine barrel in the centre and the murals depicting Dionysian pastorals, have been integrated, so gaining an even stronger prominence than before. The simple but high-quality finish in the interior gives it an urban air of chic coolness. Gone is the stale and dusty atmosphere of this landmark restaurant – it has been replaced with stylish lounges and an elegant ambience, attracting barflies and Havana-lovers alike.

ADDRESS Kornhausplatz 18, 3000 Bern 7
TRAM or BUS to Kornhausplatz or Zytglogge
WEBSITE www.kornhaus.org
ACCESS Kornhauskeller and Kornhaus Cafe open; Forum für Medien u. Gestaltung (depending on exhibition)

J Grego & J Smolenicky/C Silvestrin/sam architekten 1997–99

J Grego & J Smolenicky/C Silvestrin/sam architekten 1997–99

Federal Alcohol Administration, Bern

The large, crisp-white building leaves the observer perplexed: is this a new building or a renovated *Neues Bauen* project? Both, in fact. In 1993, some parts were torn down and replaced by new additions. Rolf Mühlethaler, confronted with a conglomeration of buildings of varying characters and ages – an art nouveau villa, buildings from the 1890s and the anonymous post office built in 1948 – reorganised the Alcohol Administration, a government organisation long in need of centralisation. The architectural language of the post office was adopted to unify and strengthen the complex. The architect opted for a reinterpretation of a classic modernism that aimed at a coherent identity.

The white plaster walls and the penthouse replacing the old saddle roof are the most important elements. Seams between old and new are made visible by two large glass-block openings in the façade and the subtle differentiation of window types – punched windows in the old building and long strip windows in the additions – where the façades are relieved of their supporting function. Mühlethaler has adapted and not merely adopted the forms and tropes of the *Neues Bauen*. His obvious earnestness avoids a nostalgic homage to the architecture of the 1920s. His concomitant rationalism reflects a search for the distilled essence of an architecture that eliminates all extraneous elements.

ADDRESS Länggassestrasse 33, 3012 Bern
CLIENT Federal Alcohol Administration
STRUCTURAL ENGINEERING H P Stocker & Partner AG, Bern
COST SF22.5 million
SIZE 4872 square metres
TRAIN to Bern main station, then BUS 12 in direction Länggasse
ACCESS none; visible from the street

Rolf Mühlethaler 1990–94

Rolf Mühlethaler 1990–94

Unitobler, Bern

The Tobler chocolate factory buildings, formerly home to Switzerland's most famous chocolate bar, Toblerone, are now part of the University of Bern. In 1982, when the canton decided to buy the factory, plans were well underway to move some departments out of the city onto a campus at the periphery. At that time the idea of preserving former industrial sites was still new, and it was a lucky coincidence that the factory was near the university. Plans for the new campus were abandoned and the factory became the new home to the liberal arts department.

The Tobler factory had been adapted and extended numerous times over its century-old history. The latest transformation involved renovations, extensions and the addition of new elements. It was impossible to follow a singular overall design, but the architects maintained the character of the factory while transforming it into a modern institution. The two most important additions are the main library in the now-covered inner court and a new annex for auditoriums.

While Bern never had the impressive industrial architecture of cities such as Winterthur or Baden, here earlier than elsewhere it recognised the importance of preserving its architectural heritage. Unitobler, and the positive effect it has had on the neighbourhood, is a successful example of a how the transformation of already existing structures can bring new life into the city.

ADDRESS Länggassstrasse 49, 3012 Bern
CLIENT Canton of Bern, Urs Hettich
STRUCTURAL ENGINEERING Moor Hauser & Partner AG, Bern
TRAIN to Bern main station, then BUS 12 to Unitobler
ACCESS Monday to Friday, 8.00–18.00; Saturday, 8.00–12.00

P Clémençon, D Herren, A Roost 1989–93

P Clémençon, D Herren, A Roost 1989–93

Japanese Embassy, Bern

This site, home of the Japanese Embassy since 1996, was formerly occupied by a stately farm house, which had burned down. Replacing its prominent presence, the embassy, together with the adjacent half-timbered restaurant, refers to the former gateway along this historic avenue leading into the centre of Bern.

The design, like so often in Switzerland, closely follows the classic language of modernism and accordingly it combines glass, metal and concrete. The interior organisation is structured into two main sections: all representational functions such as the lobby, foyer, reception hall as well as the offices of the ambassador are situated along the main road. The embassy's most important rooms are characterised by generous transparent glass surfaces between tall concrete walls. All remaining functions and offices are placed in a disconcerting three-storey volume situated at the back, facing south and overlooking the adjacent park. Moveable panels constructed from a strip-metal grid act as a sunscreen as well as a security device. The fairly complex programmatic requirements are structured and applied in such a way that the interior organisation is clearly recognisable from the outside.

ADDRESS Engestrasse 53, 3012 Bern
CLIENT Government of Japan
STRUCTURAL ENGINEERING Emch & Berger AG, Bern
COST SFI2 million
SIZE 1910 square metres
TRAIN to Bern main station, then BUS 21 to Bremgarten 'Innere Enge'
ACCESS none; visible from the street

Gartenmann Werren Jöhri Architekten, AG 1994–96

Gartenmann Werren Jöhri Architekten, AG 1994–96

Vocational Training Centre, Bern

The new entrance building of the Centre is at the northern end of the existing long shed hall of the former spinning mill. The whole complex stands wedged between two streets, the entrance facing the intersection. The compact block contains the library, administration offices, workshops and research labs, and is only connected to the older factory on the lower level. Owing to the sloping site the main entrance was placed on the intermediate level. It divides the building into the publicly accessible two upper floors with lobby and library and the lower floor containing the work spaces and labs. The spacious foyer organises the interior, and large windows overlooking the sheds emphasise the visual connection between old and new. Natural light enters the top floor through a system of hidden sheds as well as the upper glazed section stretching the full width of the library.

An additional feature of this clean-cut design is its colour concept, which the architects developed in collaboration with artist Elisabeth Arpagaus. The addition of pigments to the liquid concrete during the mixing process accounts for a special intensity and depth, and the necessary lining of the casting moulds with fine fabric gives the walls a canvas-like structure. The earthy colours derive from various test drills performed on the site prior to construction.

ADDRESS Felsenaustrasse 17, 3004 Bern
CLIENT City of Bern
COST SF8.5 million
SIZE 4040 square metres
BUS 20 to Felsenaustrasse
ACCESS school hours: Monday to Friday, 9.00–17.00; Saturday morning. For further information, telephone 031 337 37 37

Marco Graber & Thomas Pulver 1999–2000

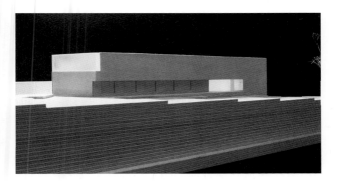

Marco Graber & Thomas Pulver 1999–2000

Vocational School, Bern

The nationwide competition for a new Gewerblich-Industrielle Berufs-schule (Vocational School) was held in the mid-1980s and Frank Geiser's Campus 2 project was chosen from about a hundred entries. Determined to take his bearings from the given location, Geiser based his project on a careful integration into the urban context. The overall design of the school complex and the arrangement of the individual volumes is based on a subtle interaction between the new buildings and the existing street grid of the neighbourhood.

The complex consists of the comb-shaped electrical engineering department positioned to the west of Jurastrasse; the elongated school containing classrooms and lecture halls to the east; and the round cafeteria in the backyard, which opens the compound up towards Lorrainepark.

The architectural vocabulary is restrained and expresses the school's utilitarian character, which engages in a technical–constructional language typical of Geiser's buildings. Yet the technical and aesthetic possibilities of glass and steel constructions are not employed in an artistic expressionism, but are always subordinate to functional requirements.

ADDRESS Lorrainestrasse 1A–G, 3013 Bern
CLIENT Baudirektoin der Stadt Bern
STRUCTURAL ENGINEERING H P Stocker & Partner AG, Bern
COST SF53 million
SIZE 17,000 square metres
BUS 20 from main station to Gewerbeschule
ACCESS school hours: Monday to Friday, 9.00–17.00

Frank Geiser 1996–98

Frank Geiser 1996–98

Office building, Zollikofen

When writing about Atelier 5 it is impossible not to mention the Siedlung Halen in Bern. Built in the late 1960s, it is has been called 'one of the most seminal pieces of land settlement built in Europe since the end of the Second World War'. Atelier 5 is still one of the best-known Swiss offices, although this early success has remained unparalleled. The office has broken considerable ground in the field of low-rise, high-density housing that followed in the wake of Halen.

Atelier 5 is not only designing housing. Much of its work, less known abroad, is not at all Corbusian and uses different vocabularies; the office building in Zollikofen is one such instance. Situated between the railway tracks and a road, it was a conscious decision to build on the outermost perimeter of the site, thereby avoiding often neglected left-over spaces. The resulting depth of the building allowed for a generous atrium separating the commercial spaces at the centre from the outer offices. The building's intelligently designed section, as well as its interior organisation, makes optimum use of the existing rail and road infrastructure. The construction and choice of materials, guided by the search for the simplest solution, give the office building a bold and compact appearance.

ADDRESS Industriestrasse 1, 3052 Zollikofen
CLIENT Mrs U Hostettler
STRUCTURAL ENGINEERING Klaus Schneider, Bachbühlach
SIZE 40,941 square metres
TRAIN to Zollikofen
CAR N1, exit Schönbühl
ACCESS by appointment only; visible from the street

Atelier 5, Architekten & Planer AG 1991

Bern and region

Atelier 5, Architekten & Planer AG 1991

Ausserholligen S-Bahn station, Bern

Far away from chic art museums, neglected public spaces generated by infrastructural nodal points are often overlooked and pushed out of the architectural conscience.

Ausserholligen is the focus of an urban development plan establishing this suburb as one of Bern's decentralised economic clusters. Every imaginable system of transport – train, bus, road and bicycle path – intersect in close proximity.

The advisory committee insisted on security as a central point of the project. The resulting concept maximises transparency on all levels while neither embellishing nor playing down the sobering reality of the surroundings. The foremost decision was to widen the underpass from a normative 4 to 12 metres. It took fierce battles to convince the SBB to allow such a divergence from its norms. The intervention consists of extending the gently sloping surface of the square into the underpass. The walls are replaced with translucent glass panels, which are illuminated at night. Ausserholligen demonstrates that the careful handling of a few fundamental elements can transform an unspectacular site into a public space that goes beyond the fulfilment of mere function.

ADDRESS Freiburgstrasse/Ladenwandweg, Bern
CLIENT SBB
STRUCTURAL ENGINEERING S M T & Partner AG/Itec Ingenieur AG, Bern
COST SFI million
ACCESS open

Rolf Mühlethaler 1995–96

Bern and region

Rolf Mühlethaler 1995–96

Cemetery extension, Bümpliz

The extension to the cemetery in Bümpliz is a beautiful and sensitive design that speaks equally of life and death. Going beyond the normative spatial requirements for cemeteries, the project carries the conviction that burial grounds can be integrated into everyday life. There are no walls segregating the grounds from the neighbourhood, and the children who use the area as a playground have proved the architects right – cemeteries do not necessarily have to be regarded as haunted grounds.

A closer look reveals how much passion and devotion went into this project, even in the smallest details. The burial grounds and the concrete walls containing the urns with the cremated remains are consciously arranged geometrically. This rigidity is opposed by the free forms of vegetal growth leaving behind traces of the passage of time. Symbols of life and death – such as the ponds alluding to the source of life, as well as to Lethe, the river of oblivion – can be encountered throughout. This serene place invites you to rest and reflect.

ADDRESS Heimstrasse/Zypressenstrasse, Bümpliz
CLIENT City of Bern
STRUCTURAL ENGINEERING Ernst Ihle, Bern
COST SF4.5 million
SIZE 16,500 square metres
TRAIN to Bern main station, then BUS 13 to the end of the line
ACCESS daytime only

Ueli Schweizer, Walter Hunziker 1987–95

Ueli Schweizer, Walter Hunziker 1987–95

Kindergarden Morillon, Bern

Bern seems to have been struggling somewhat to breathe new life into its architectural scene. Kindergarten Morillon lies in the outskirts of the city and is one of the few refreshing projects of recent years. It is situated amid anonymous high-rise buildings, neatly cut lawns and residential car parks. The inherent difference in scale between the adjacent residential blocks and the much smaller new building was dealt with in a simple but witty way. Bauart Architekten avoided a boring and isolated box and practically stretched the building's side walls until it took on the form of a kindergarten-ranch laying claim to the full plot. The wooden construction clad in crude larch wood gives the building a low-cost but integral appearance in the monotonous 1970s neighbourhood. Differentiations in the treatment of the windows show the architects' consideration for the children who predominantly use the complex: the long-framed window slit stretching along the façade is positioned at the height of a 5-year-old, while the windows for adults are mere cut-out openings in the wooden cladding above.

ADDRESS Funkstrasse 117, 3084 Wabern-Köniz
CLIENT Direktion Gemeindebauten Köniz
STRUCTURAL ENGINEERING Weber Angehrn Meyer, Bern
COST SF955,000
SIZE 147 square metres
TRAM 9 from Bern main station to Sadrain, then a 3-minute walk
ACCESS none; visible from the street

Bauart Architekten 1994–95

Kindergarden Morillon, Bern

Bern and region

Bauart Architekten 1994–95

Holzfachschule, Biel

The Holzfachschule (School for Wood Technology) complex exemplifies how far wooden architecture has evolved in the twentieth century. The building soars far above the cuckoo-clock architecture of the school's main block, built in the national-romantic style of the turn of the nineteenth century.

The most significant aspect of Meili & Peter's contemporary interpretation lies in the construction. Using large-span wood technology, the building parts from classic timber construction and breaks free of its inherently restrictive hierarchy of dimensions and divisions, and the pettiness normally associated with it.

MH/TH Your building makes a very strong statement. It seems that you have explicitly thrown all preconceived notions of wood architecture overboard.

Marcel Meili The fundamental formal interest of this thing lies ultimately in its massiveness. There is still a widespread belief that wood is cosy, delicate and light – and here it is the exact opposite. By its sheer size the annex restructures the whole complex and at the same time reverses the relationship to the old school. It now looks as if the old school is attached to the annex.

The old buildings become completely dominated. That is purely a relational problem of large and small. But, of course, there are many other aspects that are related to the building's construction and which are relatively complicated. The competition brief asked for a building entirely made of wood. To pass fire regulations with a four-storey wooden building is incredibly problematic. We had to fulfil an endless number of requirements. Our aim was to keep the construction clear and concise, while avoiding the additive system of traditional wood

M Meili and M Peter 1996–99

M Meili and M Peter 1996–99

construction with its inherent restricting dimensions. Due to new technologies like lamination techniques, wood can become a much more homogenous, massive material. So, for the walls, we developed load-bearing frames that can be stacked on top of each other. Prefabricated floor elements incorporate primary and secondary construction, fireproofing and form work all in one. We have developed this as a prototype. The supporting structure is nothing new as such. We just developed an existing system a little further. But this allowed us to reach dimensions that are unusual for wooden construction.

MH/TH Your buildings always appear to have a 'tight form', which often has a strong expressive character. This is maybe most visible in your bridge in Murau, Austria (1995).

MM The expressive character is not our goal as such. I much prefer the description of tight form. To convey such a tight form is something we try to achieve in all of our buildings. It's the search for an unalterable condition where the forms and all elements explain themselves out of their own inner logic. When this is achieved, both context and form reach an autonomous unity. I consider this to be situated at the core of the architectural problem.

ADDRESS SISH Holzfachschule, Solothurnerstrasse 102, 2504 Biel
CLIENT Hochbauamt Canton of Bern
STRUCTURAL ENGINEERING Branger & Conzett, Chur
COST SF35 million
SIZE 17,100 square metres
BUS 1 to Biel-Bözingen
ACCESS by appointment only

M Meili and M Peter 1996–99

M Meili and M Peter 1996–99

Pasqu'Art, Biel

Simple geometry and bold forms have become the hallmark for the internationally renowned practice of Diener & Diener, which won the competition for the renovation and extension of the new contemporary art museum in Biel. It is the practice's second commission for an art space, having built the Gmurzynska gallery in Cologne in 1990.

The integration of the new wing with the nineteenth-century former hospital offers a compelling solution. The pre-existing staircase forms the crucial link between new and old, providing horizontal connections between the exhibition spaces of both buildings. The granite-clad cube is read as an independent volume, standing out against the classicist building. The stone façade forcefully contrasts the rhythmical exterior of the hospital, while the new wing's clerestory glazing on the ground floor seems fragile compared with the stoney base of the old building.

The dynamic balance of this project is achieved not only through its outward expression, but also through the different characteristics and sequences of the individual exhibition rooms. The play of light and materials, as well as the directness of this modest composition, puts architecture in the service of the art exhibits and not vice versa.

ADDRESS Seevorstadt 71, 2501 Biel
CLIENT Stiftung Centre Pasqu'Art
LANDSCAPE ARCHITECT Kienast Vogt Partners, Zürich
COST SFI0.5 million (including landscaping)
SIZE 3837 square metres
TRAIN to Biel, then a 6-minute walk
WEBSITE www.pasquart.ch
ACCESS Tuesday to Friday, 14.00–18.00; Saturday and Sunday, 11.00–18.00; telephone 032 322 55 86

Diener & Diener 1998–99

Bern and region

Diener & Diener 1998–99

Pfrundscheune, Meiringen

The free-standing wooden barn was built in the eighteenth century to store the church prebends (the tithe from the parish) and its livestock. The changes and alterations needed to transform it into a mortuary had to be kept to a minimum due to the barn's historical value. The idea of a detached glass skin on the interior was developed until the architects arrived at a cube-like volume, which rests inside the hollowed timber construction. The cube takes up the material's dividing line of the outer shell, splitting it into solid lower walls and a fully glazed upper section, so offering an uninhibited view of the imposing rafters of the traditional hipped-roof construction. Hardly anything is visible from the outside, but once inside the mortuary visitors are in an enclosure that provides a serene place for contemplation alluding to the fragility of existence. Dimmed natural light is diffused through the gaps between the wooden planks and it shimmers through the large apse-like recess clad in marble. Depending on the light conditions, the 11-millimetre-thin marble panels in the openings of the former large barn doors become transparent or opaque.

ADDRESS Kirchgasse 19, 3860 Meiringen
CLIENT Gemeindeverband, Begräbnisbezirk, Meiringen
STRUCTURAL ENGINEERING Mätzener & Wyss, Meiringen
COST SF620,000
SIZE 98 square metres
TRAIN from Interlaken or Lucerne to Brünigtrain, then a 5-minute walk
ACCESS keys can be obtained from the sexton at Kirchgasse 19

Bysaeth & Linke 1993–95

Bysaeth & Linke 1993–95

Signal box

Plain dark concrete walls give this signal box an introverted 'cool' beauty that makes absolutely no reference to its surroundings. Morger & Degelo's use of lo-tech construction to shelter hi-tech electronic equipment won the competition, which asked for a prototypical design that could be easily reproduced and erected in many locations along the railway tracks. As with many of their earlier projects, the architects worked with prefabricated elements and a technique of simplification which is refreshingly banal and straightforward, yet at the same time is radical. The prefabricated wall panels are 60 centimetres thick and filled with sand and aerated clay. The floor slab is 120 centimetres thick and contains the fill from the building's excavation. Making use of the walls' thermal storage capacity and the heat generated by the electrical equipment, the building can do without a heating device and guarantees a maximum temperature of 32°C at all times. Ventilation and the minimal amount of natural light needed for repair work are achieved by means of rooflights resembling periscopes.

ADDRESS train stations Arnegg/Murgenthal/Onnens-Bonvillars, Basel
CLIENT SBB
STRUCTURAL ENGINEERING Aerni & Aerni, Zürich
TRAIN any train to Basel
ACCESS none; visible from the platforms

Morger & Degelo 1995–98

Signal box

Morger & Degelo 1995–98

Romandie

Transjurane

How does an architect react to the challenge of constructing a landscape? In the 1980s, architect Rino Tami decisively shaped the visual appearance of the road leading to Ticino. In close collaboration with civil engineers, he gave it a remarkable aesthetic quality – something that was almost unnoticed at the time. Generally, such infrastructural interventions were not thought of part of architecture's remit and its importance was only discovered retrospectively.

Architects Flora Ruchat-Roncati & Renato Salvi see the challenge in constructing a landscape by recognising the inherent potentials of a environment subjugated to a tectonic *tour-de-force*. The Transjurane integrates the remoter areas of the Jura mountains into the existing road network. The actual course of the road had already been decided in 1987 when a national competition called for a design for its 67 kilometres. Not only entrances to eight tunnels, but also bridge heads, support walls, over- and underpasses, service buildings, and ventilation shafts had to be designed and placed. The varying topography of the mountains did not allow a repetitive formulation for these interventions but instead required a search for the means of formal differentiation.

The tunnel entrance and ventilation shafts find their most dramatic articulation in the steep slopes of Les Gripons. Leaning closely against the hill, the somewhat zoomorphic structure looms above the tunnel. The jagged pattern on the concrete shield channels the rain water, while fresh air is drawn into the tunnels through openings on the side. On the softer slopes near Russelin Sud and Terri Nord, the ventilation shafts are articulated in a completely different way: free-standing, bird-like objects sit in the open countryside surrounded by grazing cows.

Flora Ruchat-Roncati & Renato Salvi 1998

Flora Ruchat-Roncati & Renato Salvi 1998

MH/TH It seems that more architects are involved in projects such as highways, bridges or signal boxes … which in the past were predominantly in the realm of engineers and other specialists. Are architects looking to these new fields as a result of the crisis in their own profession?

Flora Ruchat I believe that this is an evolution that has less to do with the problematic situation architects find themselves in than a general societal transformation. The increasing collaboration of various disciplines cannot be avoided. The architect is only one of many others, such as economic, agricultural or ecological experts, who has to be consulted. This interdisciplinary aspect has become an integral part of the overall process. A true aesthetic solution has to take functional aspects into account and can only be found on a much deeper level in collaboration with all disciplines involved. We must realise that with a highway you also build a whole new economic and ecological system.

MH/TH It seems that this awareness still needs to get stronger.

FR Yes, indeed. It is very difficult to grasp the extent of such a large project and all the implications involved. This form of collaboration is something with which we are still struggling today. The younger architects will have to learn to become more modest and willing to engage in a continuous process of researching, testing, and learning.

ADDRESS A16 from Delémont to Porrentruy
CLIENT Swiss Confederation/Canton of Jura

Flora Ruchat-Roncati & Renato Salvi 1998

Flora Ruchat-Roncati & Renato Salvi 1998

Cartier Factory, Villeret

Jean Nouvel's factory for the world-famous Parisian watch-maker is the most recent Cartier project that the firm's house-architect has realised in Switzerland. While the older distribution centre is located next to the highway (A1) near Fribourg, the factory is tucked away in the rolling landscapes of the Jura mountains. This agricultural region of Switzerland has long been home to the watch-making industry, and high-precision craftsmanship is deeply rooted in local tradition. When the company was looking for a new production site, the advantages of skilled labour overruled any economic reservations about the unfavourable location of a factory in an expensive, non-EC country.

The low-standing factory's most distinct feature is its enormous roof floating independently above a glass box that integrates the building comfortably into the topography of the landscape. The roof's sole function is the even dispersion of indirect light by means of lamellas into the production hall below, where subsequently glass is used for walls and roof alike. The egalitarian open-plan arrangement of the assembly hall achieves an astonishing sense of visual openness and connection with the outside. The strength of this simple building lies in its rigorous pursuit of transparency, not only in the use of materials, but also in the programmatic organisation.

ADDRESS 2613 Villeret
CLIENT CLT Horologerie SA
COST SF34 million
SIZE 3500 square metres
TRAIN to Villeret, then within walking distance
ACCESS by appointment only; telephone 032 942 9800

Jean Nouvel, Emmanuel Cattani & Associates 1990–92

Cartier Factory, Villeret

Romandie

Jean Nouvel, Emmanuel Cattani & Associates 1990–92

Corum Factory, La Chaux-de-Fonds

Like a Swiss-made clock, a label which stands for precision and high quality, this recent extension of the Corum factory complex is a hi-tech product. To the surprise of many, Corum (which usually sponsors yacht races and golf tournaments) has turned to supporting young architects. Only recent graduates were allowed to participate in the 1991 design competition for this extension, and of the 117 submissions the jury chose a proposal by recent ETH graduates Margrit Althammer and René Hochuli.

Using the analogy and metaphor of a watch, the young architects took on the challenge of constructing a building as precise as a clock. In contrast with industrial mass-production, Corum's manufacturing techniques still follow the tradition of hand-made watches that are assembled in small series. This is the reason why the individual work place had to be the main focus of the design. The new factory has a differentiated stratification of space adjusted to the respective function of each area. The watchmakers' workshops are situated along the windows of the west façade. Communal work space, such as laboratories, designing or engineering rooms, are on the middle tier. The building has two distinctly different façades: one is closed and is made of fair-faced concrete with flush windows; the other, more public face is fully glazed to reveal the interior. Transparency and intricate detailing, therefore, are the hallmarks of this building and its clarity results from the restricted choice of materials: steel, glass and concrete.

This building does indeed function with the precision of a clock. Every detail is perfect, leaving no room for questions or alternative answers. It is quite telling that in a country where the traditional art of watch-making is still strong, a similar attention to detail and precision is given to the making of architecture. Althammer & Hochuli are not the only young

Althammer & Hochuli 1993–95

Corum Factory, La Chaux-de-Fonds

Althammer & Hochuli 1993–95

9.10

architects to produce their first building in La Chaux-de-Fonds. Young Charles Edouard Jeanneret, a watch-engraver by trade, also realised his first architectural designs here, before leaving for Paris where he became better-known as Le Corbusier. If there is time, pick up a map with the Le Corbusier walking tour at the tourist office (032 919 68 95).

ADDRESS Rue du Petit Château 1, 2300 La Chaux-de-Fonds
CLIENT Corum; Ries, Bannwart & Co. SA
STRUCTURAL ENGINEERING GVH (A Vaucher), La Chaux-de-Fonds
COST SF9.5 million
SIZE 2400 square metres
BUS 4 to Hôpital
ACCESS by appointment only; telephone 032 967 06 70

Romandie

Althammer & Hochuli 1993–95

Corum Factory, La Chaux-de-Fonds

Althammer & Hochuli 1993–95

Federal Department of Statistics, Neuchâtel

The long and narrow plot contributes much to the fascination of this building, leaving the architects little choice but to follow its parameters. The north façade runs parallel to the railway tracks, while the south side follows the long curve of the street. The outside is dominated by the fully glazed façades. Slightly protruding balconies, functioning as sunshades, further accentuate the building's horizontality. Profilit glass to the north shrouds the building in a glow that changes according to different light conditions. The eye-catching concrete tower at the far end provides additional balcony space and serves as a fire escape.

The inner organisation is dominated by a spacious central court, its crescent shape being the result of a consistent linear organisation, which aligns all office spaces along the façades. The interior architecture is simple and serene and reduced to the basics.

The Swiss Federation as client needed to set an example of an architecture fulfilling the highest ecological standards. Solar panels that heat large water tanks and the use of computer-generated heat form a highly self-sufficient heating system. These, as well as the use of economical and ecological materials, are only some issues that have contributed to the building's success. Bauart Architekten has been awarded several prizes for this outstanding example of eco-architecture.

ADDRESS Espace de l'Europe 10, 2010 Neuchâtel
CLIENT Office des Constructions Federales, Lausanne
STRUCTURAL ENGINEER GVH St-Blaise SA, St-Blaise
COST SF123 million
GETTING THERE next to the train station
ACCESS during office hours

Bauart Architekten 1993–98

Romandie

Bauart Architekten 1993–98

Vocational School, Yverdon

This extension to the professional training school of Yverdon-les-Bains is an important project for the young architects. They had participated successfully in many competitions but this was their chance to realise their ideas on a larger project. Unusually, Ueli Brauen and Doris Wälchli, though both from the German-speaking region of Switzerland, set up their practice in French-speaking Lausanne.

The removal of an old atelier building made room for the new extension of the vocational school. New ateliers, a gymnasium and several classrooms are contained in the elongated, compact volume that connects all three school buildings, thereby endowing the complex a new sense of unity. The formal approach is straightforward and is based on functionality. Despite the differences expressed in the various typologies, the latest addition manages to create an overall coherence by means of stressing the common entrance zone as a joining element.

The three-storey-high circulation corridor is placed between the heavy concrete monolith containing service facilities and the light steel-and-glass workshops. A skylight extending over the full length of the building allows natural light to enter the workshops from both sides. The light-filtering metal grid and the profilit glass façade on the two lower levels contrast with the ennobled glazed façades of the third-floor classrooms.

ADDRESS Rue Roger de Guimps 41, 1400 Yverdon
CLIENT Canton of Vaud
STRUCTURAL ENGINEERING Sancha SA, Yverdon
COST SF22 million
SIZE 7000 square metres
TRAIN or BUS to Yverdon, then a 20-minute walk
ACCESS school hours: Monday to Friday, 8.00–17.00

Brauen & Wälchli 1996–98

Brauen & Wälchli 1996–98

Espace Gruyère, Bulle

Three or four times a year the farmers in the region round up their cattle and drive them to Bulle. The new market hall accommodates up to 500 animals for display and auction. Galletti & Matter faced the dilemma of how to integrate this immense hall into the city fabric.

Situated along one of the three principal access roads leading into Bulle, the market operates as an interface between the countryside, periphery and town. Two intersecting volumes, differentiated by materiality and form, compose the overall complex. Situated across the Place des Albergeux along the route to Vevey, the presentation hall protrudes onto the open square and clearly demarcates the main entrance. It is clad in copper and rises above the shed roof of the wooden exhibition hall, thereby standing out not only due to its prominent urban positioning, but also through its material articulation.

In following the client's request for the integration of alternate functions, the architects provided the structures with flexibility – the main hall transforms into an ice-rink in the winter.

ADDRESS Rue de Vevey 74, 1630 Bulle
CLIENT Espace Gruyère SA
STRUCTURAL ENGINEERING Dorthe & Gex, Bulle
COST SF23 million
SIZE 11,000 square metres
TRAIN to Bulle, then a 10-minute walk
ACCESS hours vary according to season

Galletti & Matter 1996–98

Romandie

Galletti & Matter 1996–98

Hotel Cornavin extension, Geneva

By 1990, Hotel Cornavin, which dates from the 1930s, was in need of considerable renovation. Providing the pretext to change and extend the original construction, the aim was to create a new architectural experience using the full potential of this centrally located building as well as to make a contribution to the urban regeneration of the city centre.

The stylish three-storey addition with its fully glazed façades, oval perforated eaves and slender steel posts completely changed the character of the old historicist hotel. Attaching the elevators to the exterior of the building allowed for more space on the inside and a new panoramic experience of the city as visitors are lifted up to the eighth floor. Standing in the fully glazed two-storey dining hall, visitors are offered a spectacular view over the roofscape of Geneva, Lac Leman and the Alps.

The new hotel rooms with their large floor-to-ceiling windows and aligned beds orientate themselves towards the landscape. Elements such as the minimal design furniture and translucent bathroom glass walls endow these rooms with a serene atmosphere quite different from the average high-end hotel room.

ADDRESS Place Cornavin, 1201 Geneva; tel.: 022 716 12 12
CLIENT G and M Fassbind, Fassbind Hotels
STRUCTURAL ENGINEER M Paquet
COST SF20 million
GETTING THERE next to Genève-Cornavin train station
ACCESS open

Devanthéry & Lamunière 1996–99

Devanthéry & Lamunière 1996–99

School, Grand-Saconnex

The protruding concrete beam lies on top of two stony volumes that form the backbone to both the primary school and the new leisure centre of Grand-Saconnex. The stocky buildings are accessed from the central space under the massive beam. Stretching over the length of the complex, the rectangular openings in the beam act as skylights, diffusing natural light into the hallway. The rhythmical shadows cast on to the smooth concrete by the sun constantly alter the atmosphere in the corridor.

The otherwise tightly controlled and constrained volume of the complex is broken up on the façade facing the garden. Rooms containing the workshops are turned outward, cut at a 45-degree angle and opened up on to the large terrace. The stony character of both the terrace and walls and the wide open landscape radiate calmness and evoke associations with the architecture of the American Louis Kahn.

The sensuous, uneven quartzite façade results from the stone being split perpendicular to its geological layering, but a closer look reveals that the entire building is clad with precast elements. The cut-out quartzite slabs were placed at the bottom of the different moulds and filled with concrete. The seemingly simple and straightforward appearance actually demanded highly complicated construction drawings: the cladding alone required about 250 types of precast elements.

ADDRESS Route de Colovrex 31, 1218 Grand-Saconnex
CLIENT Community of Grand-Saconnex
STRUCTURAL ENGINEERING Cêtre, Nusbaumer, Schreyer, Ing. Civil
COST SF13.5 million
SIZE 6200 square metres
BUS 4/44 from Geneva to Grand-Saconnex
ACCESS school hours: 9.00–17.00

Devanthéry & Lamunière 1993–95

Devanthéry & Lamunière 1993–95

European Football Headquarters, Nyon

The atmosphere and light conditions of the lake with the towering mountains as backdrop are in constant flux, so providing spectacular views. After several relocations over the past decades, UEFA was lucky to be offered these grounds on the lakeshore by the community of Nyon.

The building captures the surrounding landscape from every possible angle: Mont Blanc and Lake Geneva to the south and the Jura mountain range to the north. Glass, aluminium and stone compose the building's surfaces, diffusing the changing light conditions by their different reflective capacities. The horizontal cantilevering slabs define the three floors and give the building a floating appearance.

Visitors enter on the intermediate level by two bridges into the open entrance halls. Multi-functional office spaces are housed in the upper two floors, while the lower floor contains public programmes such as the auditorium, executive committee room, court room, exhibition gallery and dining rooms.

The architectural projects Patrick Berger is best known for are the imaginative restoration of the Viaduct Daumesnil and the famous Parc André-Citroën, both in Paris. The French architect works and teaches in Paris as well as in Lausanne.

ADDRESS La Colline, Route de Genève 46, 1260 Nyon
CLIENT Union des Associations Européennes de Football (UEFA)
SIZE 10,000 square metres
TRAIN to Nyon, then BUS 4 to Rive Piscine
ACCESS lobby and exhibition space; telephone 022 994 44 44

Patrick Berger 1996–99

Patrick Berger 1996–99

La Longeraie hotel and convention centre, Morges

In this project for the conversion of a complex of rural buildings next to a church to a hotel and conference centre, Miroslav Šik exposed and then intensified the inherent spatial quality of the site, giving it precedence over all individual interventions. The result is a strong and familiar spatial experience – powerfully evoking the feeling that the space has always been there – that could not have been done in any other way.

MH/TH It was not possible for us to distinguish between the old and the new. Did you consciously work towards this fusion?

Miroslav Šik In La Longeraie I was confronted with six different buildings from various periods. The exterior spaces had to be imagined/visualised underneath the chaotic surface. It was clear that I had to work towards a unification. The fusion created an order and through this order spaces started to emerge. Until then each building had a different silhouette and style, different windows, horrible colours. I aligned all windows, for example. Through that something emerged that had already been there and eventually it got stronger and stronger. You take things away, change, move, unify the façade all around and the spatial configuration becomes powerful. If I would have left them as four buildings representing distinctly different traditions, it would not have been possible to create an ambience. All other contestants in the competition tore everything down. At first sight it seemed that this chaos would not give much. From the very beginning, however, I was determined to preserve the church as it was.

The church for me is a valuable representative of Swiss architecture from the 1940s, an important chapter that is now under threat ....

MH/TH It seems that ... the exterior skin was the most important element.

Miroslav Šik 1993–95

La Longeraie hotel and convention centre, Morges

Miroslav Šik 1993–95

MŠ No, I would always talk of the exterior space, not the skin.

MH/TH You once mentioned that Switzerland as a country is already built, and architecture has become a question of recycling ….

MŠ Yes, we actually have to deal with this premise, irrespective of us liking it or not. We have to develop themes in a different way. I can approach the way my colleagues from modernism do it, by tearing down as much as possible. Recycling on the other hand forces us to differentiate much more; I am convinced that the value of history varies – but it also goes in cycles. I love an ensemble where different things somehow grow together. I don't get anywhere if I think in 'thematic boxes'; in transparency, carrying structure, division, materials, etc. Recycling means finding those aspects in the old which are still full of life or which can take on a completely new function. Don't mix this up with nostalgia, it is much more about respect for something tried and tested and I hesitate unblinkingly to throw things overboard just because they may not be in fashion any more.

ADDRESS La Longeraie, 1110 Morges
CLIENT Catholic Church Vaud
STRUCTURAL ENGINEERING Matter Ing. SA, Lausanne
COST SFI1 million
SIZE 16,465 cubic metres
TRAIN to La Gottaz in direction Bulle, first stop after Morges
ACCESS hotel open

Miroslav Sik 1993–95

La Longeraie hotel and convention centre, Morges

Miroslav Sik 1993–95

Chemistry Building, Ecublens

The chemistry building stands on the western edge of the Université de Lausanne's premises, marking the boundary to the Polytechnicum. While the university is administered by the Canton de Vaud, the Polytechnicum is under the Federal Government's control. The hierarchies, and orthogonal and multicellular system of the Polytechnicum, developed in 1967, clash with the university's idea of an open campus of solitaires in a park-like landscape.

Owing to its size and location, the long rectangular volume functions as a threshold separating one urban system from the other. The building absorbs the different levels of terrain and differentiates the two long façades as a response to the contrasting built environments on either side. A single-storey structure, half sunk in the ground at a right angle, is linked to the pharmaceutical building on the university's side. Strict security requirements resulted in balconies being placed on all sides to act as escape routes. The balconies make it possible to integrate oak windows into the hi-tech façade, giving the building its distinct character.

ADDRESS University of Lausanne-Dorigny (UNIL), Avenue Forel, 1015 Lausanne
CLIENT Canton of Vaud, University Board of Construction
STRUCTURAL ENGINEERING Réalini & Bader & Associés, Ingénieurs-conseils SA
COST SF86 million
SIZE 25,000 square metres
METRO to UNIL-Sorge
ACCESS Monday to Friday, daytime

Atelier Cube 1992–94

Atelier Cube 1992–94

Administration Building, Morges

This project – the winning design of a competition held in 1993 – was praised for its sensitive urban response to the well-preserved medieval town centre of Morges. The Local Government Office – one of Lüscher's most successful project to date – fits into the site by employing a modern vocabulary of clear forms, strong colours and shimmering glass walls.

Three blocks are asymmetrically arranged on a slightly raised socle. Both the linear block facing west and the six-story curved volume facing the adjacent park contain cantonal administrative offices. All volumes are arranged around the raised, central open well, which is accessed from street level via a ramp or stair.

The most striking part of the complex is the double-skinned glass wall of the curved volume, which is the key element of the building's environmental strategy. All offices function without air-conditioning, relying instead on the fairly complicated system of vents and blinds.

Lüscher, a native of Zürich who works in Lausanne, has for a long time been committed to a hi-tech aesthetic expressed in the Lausanne-Ecublens telecommunications centre of 1994, which stands just across the street from Atelier Cube's chemistry building (page 9.28).

ADDRESS Place St Louis 4, 1110 Morges
CLIENT Caisse de Pensions de l'Etat de Vaud
STRUCTURAL ENGINEERING Edmond Sumi SA
COST SF17 million
SIZE 4611 square metres
GETTING THERE walking distance the from train station
ACCESS Monday to Friday, 8.30–11.45, 13.30–16.30

Lüscher & Partenaires 1995–97

Romandie

Lüscher & Partenaires 1995–97

School, Pully

Pully is along one of the most picturesque strips of land Romandie has to offer. The south-facing terrain covered by vineyards gradually slopes down to the expanse of Lake Léman, which is only surpassed by the panorama of the Savoy Alps. The quality of the new extension to the school lies unmistakably in its integration into and articulation of this landscape.

The extension lies parallel to the slope of the terrain between the elevated schoolyard and the lakeside. The clear-cut rectangular volume is positioned below the ledge but rises one-and-a-half storeys above the schoolyard, thereby blocking the view of the lake. The centrally placed, transparent entrance hall makes up for this loss by framing a view of the lake below. It is through this glass corridor that the lower park and lakeside are reached from above. The totality of the landscape is best experienced when climbing the exterior staircase to the roof terrace, which more than compensates for the lost view of the schoolyard.

The horizontal proportions prevalent in the existing complex are carried over to the new volume, which underline the building's careful embedding into the site. The elongated volume is articulated by two distinctly different façades. The north side acts as a wall to the courtyard, its roof line following the height of the base of the old school. This is further strengthened by the rough quartzite that confirms its adherence to the base of the existing schools with irregularly arranged openings resembling embrasures. As in the Grand-Saconnex project (page 9.20), Devanthéry & Lamunière again play with the intriguing application of prefabricated stone cladding, creating the illusion of a wall made of solid stone.

To the south the façade opens up and provides an unobstructed view of the lake. Large glass windows set in aluminium frames alternate with

Devanthéry & Lamunière 1994–96

Devanthéry & Lamunière 1994–96

green, translucent resin openings – a technology borrowed from ship building. The façade displays a regular rhythm based on the subtlety of its proportions and the alternation of its materials. The south-facing façade's variations of green in glass and resin beautifully dissolve into the cool shades of blue of the lake, air and mountainside.

ADDRESS 29 Avenue des Désertes, 1009 Pully
CLIENT Gymnase Cantonal de Chamblandes
STRUCTURAL ENGINEERING J-F Thonney
COST SF10.9 million
SIZE 4200 square metres
BUS 8 from Place St Francois, Lausanne to Chamblandes
ACCESS by appointment only

Devanthéry & Lamunière 1994–96

Devanthéry & Lamunière 1994–96

School, Fully

Steep rock cliffs, vineyards and a small classical school building characterise the unusual site for this project. Galletti & Matter situated the building on top of the redundant dam – which runs perpendicular to the contours of the landscape – built to protect the village from the torrents of spring. By erecting the main volume on its foundations, the new building emphasises the odd, angular position of the former dam and resurrects the notion of a fierce confrontation with the forces of nature.

While firmly anchored to the rock at one end, the long volume containing the classrooms juts out into the valley. The entire compound, however, is held in place by the old school's steadfast position along the main axis of the village.

By means of volume, form and layout, the school creates the boundary to the vineyards and demarcates an enclosed space. This space is at the same time protected and threatened by the domineering cliff. Set against the rocks and an existing wall, the schoolyard occupies this space and functions as the roof of the sunken gymnasium. The gym's skylights take on an almost sculptural quality and are crucial elements in the structuring of the surface.

ADDRESS Saxé town centre
CLIENT Community of Fully
STRUCTURAL ENGINEERING P Bruchez
COST SF9 million
SIZE 3200 square metres
BUS from Martigny-Leytron to Saxé
ACCESS Monday to Friday, 8.00–17.00

Galletti & Matter 1994–96

Galletti & Matter 1994–96

Train station, Sierre

This building has nothing in common with the representative train stations designed over the past century. The strength of this project lies in the subtleties and differentiated articulation of the various planes. The rather austere-looking block is rhythmically structured with a play of openings of different sizes, while the granite cladding of the main façade emphasises the solidity and sheer size of the low, elongated volume. The ground floor, with its passageways and large glazed openings, clearly demarcates the public programmes, while private office space is located on the first floor.

Also worth visiting is the Ecole de Goubing (Chemin de Collines 34), built by the same local architects in 1992.

ADDRESS Place de la Gare, 3960 Sierre
CLIENT SBB
STRUCTURAL ENGINEERING Balmer & Crettaz
COST SF8 million
SIZE 3000 square metres
TRAIN to Sierre
ACCESS 5.45–21.30

Giorla & Trautmann 1994–96

Train station, Sierre

Romandie

Giorla & Trautmann 1994–96

Index

Index

Index

Index

Index

Index

Index

Index

PICTURES by the authors, except
page 1.3, 1.5, 1.7, 4.13 Christoph Sättler
page 1.9, M Eggimann
pages 1.29, 1.31, 6.27, 6.31, Pino Musi
pages 1.35, 8.27, Diener + Diener
pages 1.37, 4.21, 8.7 Heinrich Helfenstein
page 2.3, 2.5 (bottom), Vitra
page 2.7, 2.7, Richard Bryant
page 2.11, Christian Richters
pages 2.13, 15, Margherita Spiluttini
pages 3.11, 3.37, Isa Stürm & Urs Wolf
page 3.15, Christian Kurz
page 3.17, Reinhard Zimmerman
pages 3.27, 8.3, Jasmin Grego & Joseph Smolenicky
page 3.33, Jean-Pierre Dürig
page 3.35, Marcel Meili
page 3.43, 6.41 Campi + Pessina
page 3.45, Ralph Bensberg
page 4.7, Reutimann
page 4.9, Arazebra, Helbling & Kupferschmid
page 4.15, Ralph Feiner
page 4.29 Walter Mair
page 5.3, Alain Roserens
pages 5.7, 5.59, Andrea Deplazes
pages 5.27, 5.35, 9.25, 9.25, 9.27 Christian Kerez
page 5.31, D Schwarz
pages 5.37, 5.45, Valerio Olgiati
page 5.47, Feiner
page 5.49, Bearth & Deplazes
page 6.13, Enrico Cano
page 6.15, F Hildebrand
page 6.17, 6.19, L Ortelli
page 6.25, Alberto Flammer
page 6.29, Marco D'Anna
page 6.35, Alo Zanetta
page 6.37, 6.39 Eduard Hueber
pages 7.5, 7.7 P Ruault
page 7.9, Stählin Helle Kämfer
page 7.11, Sarna Kunststoff Holding AG
page 7.13, P Brühwiler
page 7.15, Pascale Guignard & Stefan Saner
pages 8.5, 8.15, Foto Crocci - Du Fresne
page 8.9, Michael Schneeberger
page 8.11, Marco Graber & Thomas Pulver
page 8.13, Sacha Geiser
page 8.17, Daphné Iseli
page 8.29, Michel Jaussi
page 8.31, Ruedi Walti
page 9.3, 9.5 Jürg Zimmermann
page 9.13, Bauart Architekten
page 9.15, Jean-Philippe Daulte
page 9.17, F Pluchinotta
page 9.19, Devanthéry & Lamunière
page 9.23, Patrick Berger
page 9.29, Lionel Deriaz
page 9.37, Galletti + Matteq
page 9.39, Giorla & Trautmann

Switzerland: a guide to recent architecture